FEAR & LOATHING
IN MY BANK ACCOUNT

MONEY MATTERS FOR THE FINANCIALLY CHALLENGED

SEAN COUGHLAN

KOGAN PAGE

First published in 2002

Apart from any fair dealing for the purposes of research or private study, or criticism or review, as permitted under the Copyright, Designs and Patents Act 1988, this publication may only be reproduced, stored or transmitted, in any form or by any means, with the prior permission in writing of the publishers, or in the case of reprographic reproduction in accordance with the terms and licences issued by the CLA. Enquiries concerning reproduction outside these terms should be sent to the publishers at the undermentioned address:

Kogan Page Limited
120 Pentonville Road
London N1 9JN
UK

© Sean Coughlan, 2002

The right of Sean Coughlan to be identified as the author of this work has been asserted by him in accordance with the Copyright, Designs and Patents Act 1988.

British Library Cataloguing in Publication Data

A CIP record for this book is available from the British Library.

ISBN 0 7494 3737 5

Typeset by Saxon Graphics Ltd, Derby
Printed and bound in Great Britain by Clays Ltd, St Ives plc

Contents

	Introduction	**1**
1.	**Getting a grip**	**5**
	You could save money right now by...	13
	How much would you need never to work again?	14
	Modern money: bank rage	16
2.	**Credit cards – will you be my best friend?**	**19**
	Getting a good deal on credit cards	23
	Credit references: are you worthy?	28
	How do credit cards compare to other borrowing?	28
	Store cards	29
	Debit cards	29
	Gold, platinum and loser cards	30
	Card fraud	30
	Donation and supporter cards	31
	What's on the cards for cards?	32
	The psychology of credit card debt	33
	Modern money: credit card junkie	35
3.	**Mortgage hunting – the loan rangers**	**37**
	You are the customer	38
	Follow the money	40
	What are the main types of mortgage on offer?	42
	How much can you borrow?	46
	What happens if you can't keep up repayments?	47

Contents

    History lesson: how interest rates can change   47
    Information on the Internet   48
    What questions should you ask?   49
    Modern money: sandwiches and interest rates   51

4. Savings – think of it as reverse borrowing   53
    Types of saving   56
    Deposit and savings accounts   57
    Internet banks   58
    National Savings   59
    Children's accounts   59
    Individual savings accounts (ISAs)   60
    Online trading   63
    Ethical finance   65
    Clear your debts before saving?   65
    Modern money: savings? Maybe next year   67

5. Pensions – when will I see you again?   69
    Pensions are complicated and depressing   69
    Maybe pensions shouldn't be called pensions   72
    Company pensions   73
    Annuities   75
    Topping-up   76
    Group personal pensions   76
    Personal pensions   77
    Stakeholders   78
    Pensions by other means   80
    Modern money: I know I'm probably heading for the workhouse, but…   82

6. Borrowing – neither a borrower nor a lender be. Yeah, right   83
    What has all this got to do with borrowing?   83
    Know the enemy: what to look out for in a loan   86

How do different types of borrowing compare?	87
How do these loans work?	88
Credit checking	96
Modern money: why do you need money?	98

7. Insurance – the seven ages of man — 101

Motor insurance: mirror, signal, oh bugger	104
Contents insurance	106
Buildings insurance	107
Travel	108
Private health insurance	109
Life insurance	111
Endowments	113
Payment protection	114
Insurance wind-ups	114
Modern money: 'It's like there's good insurance and junk insurance'	116

8. Debt problems – till debt us do part — 119

How do we get into debt?	120
What can you do if you're in debt?	123
Consolidating debts	125
Don't feed the sharks	126
Debt warning signs	126
Modern money: the debt adviser, Sue Edwards, Citizens Advice Bureaux	127

9. Online banking – taking CTRL of your money — 129

Internet banks	132
Online accounts	133
Online share dealing	135
Online window shopping	137
Security	140
Is it just the Bank of Bloke?	142
Modern money: I can't remember what it was like before	144

10.	**Excuse me, I'd like to ask you a question**	**147**
	1. Getting a grip	147
	2. Credit cards	148
	3. Mortgages	149
	4. Savings	149
	5. Pensions	150
	6. Borrowing	151
	7. Insurance	152
	8. Debt problems	153
	9. Money online	153
	Conclusion	**155**
	Index	**161**

Money suffreth long, and is kind; money envieth not; money vaunteth not itself, is not puffed up, doth not behave unseemly, seeketh not her own, is not easily provoked, thinketh no evil; rejoiceth not in iniquity, but rejoiceth in the truth; beareth all things, believeth all things, hopeth all things, endureth all things... And now abideth faith, hope, money, these three; but the greatest of these is money.

> From *Keep the Aspidistra Flying* by George Orwell
> (adapting I Corinthians XIII)

Introduction

I've always had an uneasy relationship with money. Like suspicious neighbours, we've seen a great deal of each other, but we've never been close.

I've carried out all the usual financial transactions – mortgage, car loans, overdrafts, credit cards, insurance – but for many years these arrangements depended more on guess work than know-how. Dealing with financial companies was 'going behind enemy lines', leaving me unsure as to what I should be trying to find and what I should be avoiding.

The turning point for my troubled relationship with money came when I was asked by the *Guardian* to write a column each week about personal finance – with the commission to find out how my finances could be improved and to pass on my experiences to the readers in a way that was as accessible and demystifying as possible.

My starting point for this journey of financial self-improvement was not auspicious. I had a long and undistinguished record as Overdraft Man. I was the thirty-something with children who still had no pension, despite all the warnings that this would condemn me to old age in the workhouse. I was in sympathy with a friend who admitted he'd spent more time choosing his suit than his mortgage.

It wasn't that I didn't want to learn more about money, it was just that the information available seemed to be written in a way that made me lose the will to live – the kind of small-print-speak that yells 'Don't read me… and if you do you still won't understand'.

I was certainly not alone in my lack of understanding about how to get the most out of the little money that I had.

Survey after survey shows a great national blindspot in personal finance – and an equally great desire to find out more about the mysteries of money. We don't want to become bores with calculators – but we also don't want to be ripped off. And if we have to borrow money for a new car or a wedding, or if we want to make an investment, we don't want to feel as if we're throwing money down the drain.

This money angst becomes more urgent for many of us as we come face to face with important financial decisions. We begin to worry about having no savings, no pension and no life insurance. Mortgaged and married, we begin to wonder how to ensure that we're financially protected.

And it's usually at this point that we realize we know nothing about money. As grown ups, we think we're in control of our lives, but then discover we're asked to make big decisions on the basis of a few glossy leaflets and a five-minute phone chat with a nameless voice in a banking call centre. And where do we turn for help? The experts – people like independent financial advisers – look too much like the slick guys in suits we're afraid are taking us for a ride. So where can we go to arm ourselves with useful advice?

This book is intended as a starting point for anyone seeking to find out more about the basics of money. It isn't a training manual for frustrated accountants or for anyone who wants to chat about unit trusts at parties, it's about the everyday stuff such as credit cards, personal loans, mortgages, pensions, debt, savings, investments, children's savings, financial advisers, complaining to banks, life insurance, travel insurance, buying a new car and online banking. And even if all the questions are not answered here, this book should equip readers to ask their own questions and to cut a better deal for the specific requirements of their own finances.

As well as tackling the mechanics of money, I think it's important to face up to some of the more complex and subtle emotions that surround our dealings with banks and financial companies. Many people hate their banks – or at least have a deeply ambivalent relationship with them. We might have been made to feel small or unimportant, unwanted and unacknowledged by our bank – and when they try to offer advice, we can feel more suspicion than gratitude.

The antagonism felt by many people towards the financial services sector is as much an issue as the value of the actual products being offered. For instance, the government and the financial companies want many more people to make provisions for a personal pension on the basis that the state pension will be next to worthless in a few decades – but there is widely held consumer resistance to this, in part, research suggests, because people don't trust the companies that sell them. Even though we might be aware of the need for a personal pension, the thought of going into Spiv City to buy one can be enough to make a poverty-stricken retirement seem a reasonable alternative.

As well as looking at money in a conventional sense, we should consider more diverse perspectives. For instance, I've always thought that my problem with filling in my self-assessment tax form had more to do with psychology than finance. We might also ask how our uncertain relationship with money can make it difficult to make decisions – we often don't shop around to our own best advantage. Also, I've always been fascinated by people who can turn their backs on money and either live in a community without personal money or depend on barter and trade rather than cash.

Personal finance can easily become detached from everyday experience – entering a fantasy world in which people have financial records filed like library books where every year an investment matures and everyone knows the latest interest rates for saving and borrowing. This isn't how many of us live. But even on Planet Chaotic Reality, there are ways of making sure you give away less of your money and spend more of it on yourself.

Sadly, this book won't make you rich. If there was a conjuring trick for instant riches, this would be a much more expensive book and I wouldn't be writing it in south-east London. But it does offer ideas for taking greater control of how your money is handled, so that you're *taking charge* of your own cash rather than responding to a series of disasters.

There are no right or wrong answers when handling money because it isn't an exact science and what's right for you will depend on the type of person you are and your particular circumstances. So this isn't a rulebook and it's not pretending to have all the answers, because every individual area of personal finance could fill its own library.

If you do want to ascend to more rarefied heights, then this book can be seen as a kind of base camp. From here, you can survey the big picture and get an idea of what's possible. It might even be a view that's enjoyable.

Even serious money needn't always be serious. You can make sure you're not being ripped off in your home finances without having to approach the whole subject as if it were a session of double maths on a wet Wednesday afternoon. Money has to be seen as part of our everyday life, not an isolated activity that can be observed from afar by financial trainspotters. So this book tries to look at how people *really use* money and the problems that can arise from having too little cash or too much debt.

Even though we think of money in terms of pounds and pence, it also has an important emotional value – marriage guidance counsellors always say that money is one of the biggest sources of arguments between couples. This book looks at the emotional reactions people have to money, responding to its power and symbolic importance, as well as to the bottom line of profit and loss.

So read on for tips on saving money, how to avoid paying too much when borrowing, case studies, observations and money-related statistics to dazzle your friends. In addition, I have provided a comprehensive list of details for useful contacts. All of these should give you ideas on how to hack your way through the money jungle.

Money isn't everything, but it's not a bad start.

1
Getting a grip

We're all afraid of money. We're afraid of not having enough. We're afraid that we're not using it to our own best advantage. We're afraid of losing it. We're afraid of all the jargon and small print, in case the golden goose we think we're buying turns out to be a turkey.

Even if we don't really feel afraid of money, we're not completely confident either. Because money is something that we're not used to talking about. There's an *embarrassment* about talking too directly about money, as if money were a kind of nakedness that we want to cover up.

> How can we stop feeling so out of control?
> Maybe the first step is that we should admit how chaotic our finances can be – and *not to feel bad about it.*

Money is meant to be about brass tacks, about hard facts, but in most of our lives it's as much about emotions as economics. Of course we pretend that our financial decisions are rational. But just take a look at your credit card statement. Was that spending spree rational? Or was it something that you couldn't resist even though you knew it was a bad idea? How much do you have to show for all those years of work? And why is that everything you earn seems already earmarked for spending on bills, loans, mortgage, stuff for the children, taxes, insurance and all the other expenses that can be gathered under the heading of 'Nothing left for me then (again)'?

Financial advice usually assumes that you don't really have feelings, just economic necessities. But life doesn't have many straight lines and rules about money soon get bent out of shape.

We have such strange feelings about money. We're all meant to want more of it. But at the same time we're not meant to be greedy. We're meant to want to chase it, but never to let anyone see that we're chasing it. Even if they get a stash of money, there are people who are then consumed with guilt and have all kinds of pangs about not deserving it. And all we're talking about is currency, a system of economic exchange, paper and coins.

Look at how many euphemisms there are for money. Bread. Dough. Dosh. Spondoolicks. Mammon. Swag. Wedge. Moolah. Loot. Ackers. Shekels. Filthy lucre. The folding variety. Perhaps only sex could claim to have more ways of not saying what you mean. It suggests that there's something private and slightly furtive about money. Even though we all need it and use it, we like to be secretive about it. We don't like people to know how much we earn, we don't like to ask people directly how much they earn.

And all the time money remains one of the most important driving forces in our lives. We worry about it, we feel that we're missing something, or that we're getting it wrong somewhere. But when we decide to find out more we run into another problem. We don't know what to ask. We've never been taught.

You can spend 16 years in education, from infant school to graduation, gathering information about everything from Thomas Hardy to microbiology to French irregular verbs, but you'll never come across a lesson where they teach you how to make out a cheque or how to calculate interest on a loan.

When we go to look for a mortgage, with maybe 4,000 different mortgages to choose between, who has ever shown us what they all mean? We're chucked in the deep end with a container load of glossy leaflets and the kind of information overload that turns your brain to spam.

And how do we know if we're signing up for a disaster? People who bought into endowment mortgages a decade ago had little idea that there was much risk involved. And the people who were contributing to Equitable Life pensions had no idea of any problems on the horizon.

It's not just that financial products are complicated, there's also a feeling that they're not really giving us many clues to help. Perhaps things have improved in the last few years, with more banks and lenders providing comprehensible information. But there are still subjects that seem deliberately *designed to baffle*. If you begin to read the small print on a pension, it's as if you've waved goodbye to the English language.

This is intimidating to the ordinary punter, who wants to know but doesn't want to seem stupid by asking. So we feel our way without really knowing where we're going, using the language of money as though it were a foreign language we were learning from a phrase book.

Take a look at this example, found by the Plain English Campaign, which is a reply to a request from someone wanting to know how much pension they would be getting:

> When the added years awarded to you under the Scheme exceed 6.2/3rd years, there is a reduction of an amount equal to 30% of your redundancy payment in respect of each year (and part year) of service in excess of this. This amount is deducted from your additional lump sum, but if the said amount is greater than the additional lump sum, the outstanding balance is capitalised and deducted from the additional pension. When the added years awarded are 6 years 243 days or less there is no reduction in your compensation.

What does this mean? It means *keep your nose out* of your own money and don't ask questions. It's the world of money saying that it doesn't want to be accountable to everyone else.

It makes us feel worried that we might be making the wrong decision or that we're being taken for a ride. This sense of being out of our depth also leads to resentment and a complicated set of reactions to money. Instead of feeling that money is in our pocket, we can feel that we're in the pocket of money. Suddenly we're in our 30s, couple of kids, mortgage and money owed on the car, and we don't have any savings. We've worked for years and there's nothing to show for it except debts.

Of course, the message should be that we should take control of our money and make sure that we're making the decisions. But often it's difficult to know where to begin. Who do we ask first? Perhaps you're lucky to have an approachable bank manager – although because many of us never go into a branch, you might never have even met your manager.

And banks bring out strange feelings. They want to be like friendly uncles, with all the advertising emphasizing the feel-good factors. But many people still see them as stern headteachers, authority figures who never really treat customers as adults. A bank isn't a person, but people talk about them as though they had characters – and more particularly character faults.

Banks don't care and they never listen, people say, sounding like spurned lovers. Banks suddenly change from Mr Nice Guy to Mr Nasty. We've been loyal to a bank for 20 years and the first time we need help, they tell us to get stuffed. And so we nurse our grievances, feeling that these great unfeeling structures have set out to trample over our plans and embarrass us when we need their financial support. There are people who are driven crazy by resentment over injustices real or imagined committed by banks. If you want to watch people turn angry, get them talking about their *Bad Bank Experiences*.

But what is a bank? A big company that lends, invests and generally looks after money, mostly using automated systems. It doesn't live in a big house like a giant in a fairy story. And ultimately it sells a service, like a garage sells petrol. To extend the petrol analogy, if we go to the most expensive garage each time and always make a point of putting the wrong fuel in our engine, what's the best advice? Go somewhere else and choose a more appropriate fuel. *Take control of what you're doing.* Or instead, as we probably would with banks, we could continue going to the expensive garage and then moan in the pub about how they sold lousy petrol.

People have an emotional relationship with banks. They might have chosen the same bank as their parents, they might like the logo or the colour of the chequebook. How else can we explain that there are banks with interest rates that are 30 times lower than their competitors, but still get customers? Can you imagine if a pub sold pints at 30 times the price of the pub next door? How many customers would it get? But in banking, such differences seem to have relatively limited impact on customer preference. And the strangest part is that we're unlikely to challenge the banks that are offering the worst deals. Again, if you went into a pub and were asked for 60 quid for a pint, you might have a few suggestions of your own for the landlord.

But in the land of money we know our place – and we don't like to seem as though we're haggling, even though it's our money that is paying for all the trappings of authority that financial institutions like to acquire.

Talking about money too openly doesn't seem polite. We like to be a little covert about money, lowering our voices; like slipping the hotel porter a tip, it's all a bit awkward. We like to keep money out of sight. But it's never really out of mind.

Within relationships, money can be the great lightning conductor of anxieties. Couples argue about money like nothing else: it's one of the great friction burns of living together. How we handle money becomes a symbol for other tensions in our relationships. Whether you have a joint account or separate current accounts can become a discussion not about money but about *commitment.* Having your own money can be about wanting *independence* – even though the argument might appear to be about organizing family finances.

Who pays for what and whether it's fair is one of the great set piece bust-ups of all relationships. We've all spent time harbouring resentments and feeling that we were being ripped off. And we've all conveniently forgotten the other stuff that our partner is paying for. A good way of helping an argument to go nuclear is to suggest that you've been paying for everything for too long and you've had enough of it.

Money is *power* in a relationship, letting the possessor of money take decisions, giving them mobility and allowing them to make choices. Not having money, or depending on someone else for money, can generate feelings of being undervalued or trapped, because there's no way of buying a quick ticket out.

There is also plenty of research to show that people can be dishonest about money within a relationship. Men who don't like to admit that they've lost control of their money can be reluctant to admit to the extent of debt problems. And debt advisers report that it's sometimes only during counselling sessions that men admit to their wives how much they really owe, which must make for an interesting taxi ride home.

Surveys have shown that many women have emergency money stashed away, so that if relationships collapse and they need to escape, they have funds available. If they've had children and not been working, having some kind of independent money, away from any joint savings, can be an important psychological lifebelt. And for men, who are so anxious about commitment that they need to watch 30 television programmes at once, shovelling away a few furtive quid is a way of keeping their options open, a chance to indulge the fantasy that they're still waiting for that call of the wild.

There are also suggestions that men are more likely to set up complex networks of cash, with accounts here and there and a great deal of vagueness as to what they're all for and why they need to be kept open and separate from other family accounts. This is the financial equivalent of middle-aged men preferring the shed at the end of the garden to spending time indoors.

Of course financial eccentricity is in the eye of the beholder. What seems perfectly normal behaviour to one person will seem like the strangest practice to someone else. There are people who are compulsive record keepers, making a note of every movement in their financial lives. There are other people who operate a scorched earth policy and throw away everything from a bank as soon as it arrives.

Such traits are often reflections of how people grew up and how their family behaved towards money. There are adults who are completely guilt-tripped about money as a result of their childhoods. Parents who have used money as a means of control can pass on anxieties for generations to come. Parents who have got into difficulties with money can leave children afraid that their financial world might suddenly be snatched away. This might reveal itself as meanness or recklessness with money, or a sense of insecurity about having enough, or a need to have too much, but the roots of the problem will be in the family and not in the finances.

So what can we do to help ourselves feel that we can get a grip on our own money? How can we stop feeling so out of control?

Maybe the first step is admitting how chaotic our finances can be – and *not to feel bad about it*. Money management isn't some kind of aerobics that's going to get rid of the financial flab. A whole load of motivational nonsense isn't going to turn a low income into a fat cat salary. And for many of us, money is always going to be about stretching too little too far. So we're never going to escape the land of overdrafts, second-hand cars and loans that never seem to get paid off.

How well we can perform the financial balancing act and keep ahead of the money game is going to become more crucial in the years ahead. As never before we're going to depend on making the right decisions. With life expectancy now raising the prospect of many people living for 20 years after retirement – and the prospect of the state pension being worth very little – this is going to see millions of us living on whatever we've invested in a pension and savings. This isn't a theory, it's a certain fact, and we all need to recognize the importance of taking control of our own future welfare.

This will require a *cultural shift*, because we've never really been used to being responsible for our own financial security. But even without any hype or pretensions, we can make sure that within the context of our own money we can take charge of what we have. We can avoid the depressing black hole of debt problems. We can avoid paying more than is necessary to lenders. We can make the most of any spare cash. It might not seem like the end of the rainbow, and it might not seem as comprehensive a plan as waiting to win the lottery, but it might just work.

And one last thing. Money. *Aargh!* Or to use another longer technical term. *Aaaaargh!*

Fear and loathing in my bank account

How disorganized are your finances?

Please tick the statements that apply to you.

- Has most of your pay cheque disappeared by the end of payday? ☐
- Have you ever had to use one of those dodgy cheque-cashing services? ☐
- Have you ever had to buy the weekly food on your credit card? ☐
- Have you borrowed to pay off an earlier loan? ☐
- Is the interest rate on your mortgage a mystery to you? ☐
- Do you interpret 'outstanding balance' as a compliment? ☐
- If you lost your job would you be broke in a month? ☐
- Is your car worth less than the amount you still owe on the car loan? ☐
- Are you afraid of the post? ☐

If you've said yes to more than three of these, it means two things. First, that you are no stranger to money chaos. Second, that this is the same money chaos that afflicts most of the adult population. If you've said yes to all of these questions, I think I saw you in the pub last night, trying to scrounge drinks.

You could save money right now by…

When it comes to getting financial advice, you can usually depend on being shown an inky bar chart, with tiny letters at the end of each column and a key showing different types of shading that never seems to have an equivalent in the chart.

This is pointed to as explaining something or other and generally implying that if you weren't so idle and feckless it would be the key to your future prosperity. It has the benefit of looking rather impressively mathematical, which always suggests someone telling you something about money that you're never going to understand.

So I'm afraid there is no bar chart or graphic showing you as a top hat from the Monopoly board or a pound coin turned into a pie chart. Not least because I don't know how much you earn, how much you owe, how much you pretend to earn, or how much you worry about it all. But it is possible in almost every case, without any resort to over-complex statistics, to save money almost immediately. It's like giving yourself a pay rise.

- If you owe any money on a *credit card,* check the interest rate. Then look in the personal finance pages of a newspaper or look up a Web site such as www.moneyfacts.co.uk and see if there is a card with a cheaper rate. There almost certainly will be, if only for an introductory six-month offer. Ring the card provider with the cheaper interest rate and ask about transferring your balance. It is very easy and straightforward and is a way of giving yourself money for very little effort.
- If you have a *mortgage,* check how much you are paying and then look at the best rates on offer elsewhere. Moving mortgages between lenders is easier than ever before, and again a few phone calls can be a short step to saving a considerable amount of money. If you're paying over the odds in interest, nobody is going to be bothered about this apart from you. And if you choose to pay more than necessary all your life, no one is going

to stop you. But within a day, you can take steps to save money every month on your mortgage.

- If you have a deposit account, look to see how much you're *earning in interest* and check how this compares with other offers. If you've had this account for a number of years, it could be something of a dinosaur. If you have access to the Internet, consider the above-average interest rates available from Internet bank accounts. And make use of tax-free investments such as Individual Savings Accounts (ISAs).
- Look at all your *utility and fuel bills* and consider other cheaper providers, or deals where there are discounts for combined services, such as getting your gas and electricity from the same provider. If you use your phone for many international calls, there are a number of discount phone companies that offer considerable savings on calls, without having to change your number or close any other accounts.

How much would you need never to work again?

This is the kind of question that financial advice really needs to address. What size of lottery win would you need to say goodbye to the sad world of work? The answer according to financial advisers is about £1 million – but the twist to the story is that this would yield about £50,000 per year.

If you had a million and spent a million, buying a flash house and a few holidays, you'd still need to have an income. So you need to protect the capital sum, by investing it in a way that would not expose it to undue risk, but would still generate a regular income.

So if you had the mythical million, without having to get out of bed and without losing control of the original investment, you could expect a pre-tax income of about £4,200 a month. It's not exactly the lifestyle of the rich and famous, but it's better than getting the train to work every morning. On the downside, since this plan would involve not blowing the million, you would still need to sign up for the usual wallet-emptying arrangements that afflict ordinary wage slave life, such as mortgages and car loans.

So perhaps we need to revise our greed upwards: £1 million to invest and another £1 million for some power shopping and a change of address. Don't settle for anything less.

Ten things about money to dazzle your friends

- One and a half million households have no bank accounts.

- Each year £1.8 billion is withdrawn from cashpoints.

- Fifty-two per cent of adults have credit or charge cards.

- In 2000, £5.4 trillion was traded through the London Stock Exchange.

- The average debt per household is £10,700.

- The average household income is £23,200.

- The highest average household income is in Surrey.

- Chrometophobia is the fear of money.

- Six million households have no contents insurance.

- The shortfall in household savings is £27 billion.

Fear and loathing in my bank account

Modern money: bank rage

Sarah, aged 32, recalls her bad experience with a bank:

> I'm sure the bank had no idea how angry it made me. It wasn't about money any more. It was about feeling that they thought they could walk all over me. And at the same time I was meant to be their customer, I was the one they were meant to be helping.
>
> Even though it's three years ago, I can still feel angry thinking about it. And really, if you think about it in the cold light of day, it was about nothing. It began when they charged me £10 for a letter telling me that I had broken my overdraft limit. To cut a long story short, I disagreed because the overdraft limit had been increased. Or at least I thought it had. But what really soured all this was their attitude, their 'the customer is always wrong' approach.
>
> When I protested, their reaction was to tell me I was wrong and to threaten me with more penalties. It was as if they were saying they were going to help themselves to as much of my money as they wanted. My current account was empty, which was my fault, but there was plenty in the deposit account, so they knew I had funds.
>
> I thought that this would be easy to sort out over the phone or I could call in for a quick chat, but they really didn't want to know. And I suddenly felt very small and it felt as though they couldn't care less whether I was their customer or not. From their perspective, that was probably right, because I'm never going to be investing millions with them, I'll always be just an ordinary customer.
>
> What I remember most was how angry and frustrated I was left feeling. It was that powerless rage that I could last remember from when I was a child. I'm sure my friends must have been sick of hearing about it, but I was incandescent. It felt like I'd been robbed, and every time I turned on the television there was an advert for the bank showing them as these people who couldn't do enough to help.
>
> It ended up with some bad tempered letters and a few messy phone calls where I never really got to speak to anyone who could help. And I felt as though they had switched off and saw me as making a fuss about nothing. It was only a £10 letter and some interest for the days before

more funds went into the account, but it was my money. But what made me really angry was that they could be so high handed about the whole question. It made me feel as though my money wasn't really safe with them.

I know this isn't a very dramatic story, not one of those where hundreds of thousands of pounds go missing and there are letters from the managing director, but it changed my dealings with banks. I'd been with my bank since I was a child, it was the same bank as my parents, and it felt strange to suddenly be made to feel like the enemy.

I switched banks, which felt like quite a wrench at the time, and so far I've not had any problems. I think I use banks differently now, perhaps more impersonally. As well as a current account with a high street bank, I've got a high interest Internet bank account, and I think that if I was unhappy with either of these banks, I'd have no hesitation about moving again.

2

Credit cards – will you be my best friend?

People come and go, friends leave you, but there's always your little plastic buddy in your wallet. Even when you don't have any money, he'll buy you a drink or take you shopping or put you on the plane for an emergency holiday.

Is that how we think about credit cards? We must have a high opinion of them because they're popular as never before. There are now *over 100 million cards in circulation* – put end-to-end this would

> **When we're in spending mode a credit card is the magic pocket that never empties**, it's our get out of jail free card.

stretch to 40 laps of the M25, a huge motorway of plastic temptation. And we're not shy about using them. The current rate of spending on cards is over £5,000 *a second* and in 2001, for the first time ever, half the spending in Britain's high streets was on plastic rather in cash.

So why have we become so keen on the cards? And why do we allow ourselves to pay out so much interest on credit cards? And why do we see the Mr Nice Guy side of cards and forget the nightmare that comes with credit card debt?

In the first instance, we like cards because they make life easier. Buying air flights or cinema tickets over the phone, or shopping on the Internet, is more straightforward using a credit or debit card than messing about with cheques.

And for big purchases people seem to prefer to pay on the plastic rather than to hand over wads of crumpled notes. If you do pay in cash for anything costing much more than a hundred quid, I've noticed that cashiers give you that look that says, 'You've had your card cut up then?'

But why have credit cards become many people's favourite form of borrowing? In the cold light of day, even though we use them as an alternative to cash, a credit card is just another form of borrowing.

When we're in spending mode a credit card is *the magic pocket that never empties,* it's our get out of jail free card. It lets us spend money when we don't have the cash. It lets us spend money we don't even have in our bank accounts. And if it's a really good night, it lets us spend money that we won't be earning for several months ahead. Altogether, in a single year, we can collectively put £163 *billion* through our cards.

We don't seem to think about credit cards in the same way that we think about other types of borrowing. If you were on holiday and – overcome by a mixture of sangria and heat exhaustion – you decided to buy a load of new clothes, you wouldn't start arranging a personal loan. That would seem ridiculous. That would be like real borrowing, with repayments and interest rates and all the rest of it. But you might whip out the credit card. And *putting it on the card feels like a way of putting it off,* postponing the point at which you'll have to worry about paying.

It's as though we have a different kind of relationship with credit cards than we have with cash. And if you talk to people about their credit cards you soon realize that we have feelings about credit cards. Credit cards can give people a sense of status, saying they've arrived in the adult world. Rather than pulling out more notes than a Monopoly champion, they can take pleasure from their souped-up platinum drop-dead high-income credit card. When you hear about shopping therapy, it's not people going around the shops with a brown envelope full of their wages. They go binge shopping with their flexible friends, swiping the credit card back and forth faster than a sushi chef on speed. And the card is their special assistant in all this spending, it's their source of spending power, their *cash muscle*. It gives them a kind of high.

Professor Jan Pahl at the University of Kent has carried out research into how people reach financial decisions and how these decisions can be influenced by social attitudes and personal feelings about money. She quotes a businessman's description of how he used his gold card:

> Depending on who I'm with, if I want to vaguely impress them, I'll get out the gold card. If they get out their gold card and we're splitting the meal, then I whack mine on the table and that gives some kind of credibility I suppose.

Is this about money or is this a baboon showing us his brightly coloured backside? And what 'credibility' does he imagine comes with a gold card?

Credit cards can also make people feel *safe*, like a little plastic lifebelt, so that even if they never get beyond the shallow waters of their credit limit, they feel that if they really needed it, they could use the card to bring them home safely or to cover some unforeseen danger.

Or they might feel a kind of *hatred* for this little plastic slice of temptation. 'It's got me into so much trouble,' they say, as if the credit card went on spending sprees without them. Even though the bank account was running on empty and there were no more pennies in the jar, they've gone out partying with the credit card and spent next month's money. And who gets the blame? That card. Should have chopped it up years ago. Charging a fortune in interest. Never pay it off. Probably have to sign up for another card before the holidays.

There are also people who feel *guilty* about credit cards – and talk about their credit habit as if it were an eating disorder. They stack on the pounds, often in a way that almost seems compulsive, until it becomes a problem. And then they feel terrible about themselves – and promise to become total credit card puritans, putting huge efforts into paying them off, going without luxuries to cut back on the debt, as though punishing themselves for their excess. But then no sooner will they have paid everything off than the whole cycle begins again – and out go the sackcloth and ashes and it's back to spend, spend, spend, then guilt, guilt, guilt and so on.

Now with credit cards playing such a complex part in the great soap opera of our lives, it might be no great surprise that we don't behave entirely rationally in our borrowing. If we were being sensible about it, we would pay off all our credit card bills each month and only spend what we could afford to repay. That way there would be no need to worry about interest rates and all you'd ever pay would be a few charges. But that isn't quite how it works. And at any one time we have a total credit card debt of about £20 billion and an average balance of over £600 per card. Which means many of us are paying a hefty stack of interest each month.

Jan Pahl's research came across another credit card holder who had got into difficulties with debt. This is how she described how she always spent to the maximum limit of her credit allowance:

> You get to your limit of maybe £1,500 and as you get there… then they write and say to you, 'We've upped your limit to £2,500.' And you think, ooh, I've got a bit more to spend. And then you spend that bit more.

Not clearing your card every month means paying a penalty in interest. But a much bigger cost is attached if credit card borrowing gets completely out of hand. Every year, Citizens Advice Bureaux see hundreds of thousands of people with credit card problems, who have to face the slow uphill struggle to pay back creditors and to rebuild their financial lives. It's a massive problem, the dark underbelly of the credit culture.

You can see how it happens all too easily. First you begin to let the balance increase each month, this drifts upwards over time, and then you might even get a second card, and even though you're planning to clear them both, you'll put that off until after Christmas or when you're back from holiday. Maybe you owe a few thousand altogether, too much to pay off all at once, but not enough to really worry about.

And then you hit an iceberg, losing your job or becoming ill or whatever, and suddenly there's no money for the repayments. And if you start missing repayments, the bill starts going haywire like a runaway taxi meter. You're in trouble and you'll probably need help to get out. There is advice available, such as the National Debtline (0800 808 4000) and the Consumer Credit Counselling Service (0800 138 1111), but there are *no easy answers* – and it's going to be a tough road back and you're going to be left with a poor credit record, which is going to make borrowing more expensive and more difficult in the future.

Contrary to all kinds of stereotypes about women, shopping and credit cards, men on average have larger credit card debts than women. And men are also more likely to lie about the extent of their credit card bills, because men find it difficult to accept that they have lost the plot with their borrowing.

Young people are also more likely to run into credit card problems. While older people still feel a certain reluctance to get into debt, young people have grown up in an era of easy credit, where they're targeted as potential borrowers from as soon as they leave school. Students who no longer receive a grant are now borrowing against credit cards as a matter of course – and are then facing long months of repayments after they graduate.

I have to confess to making several contributions to the national over-population of cards. But I'm getting tired of carrying more cards than a Mississippi steamboat gambler, with a wallet stuffed with loyalty cards, bank cards, store cards and credit cards. So if I want to get rid of all my cards except one, how should I find the right card for me? And how can I make sure I get a good deal?

Getting a good deal on credit cards

Every week a new credit card seems to be launched, promoted not just as a card for buying things but as a lifestyle in plastic. There are aggressively promoted low interest rate cards and there are cards which sell themselves as matching your interests, whether it's fundraising for a charity that you support or a football team.

There are over 1,500 cards on the market at present, and forgetting the pretty pictures on the front, what are the distinguishing features that are worth considering? There are three key factors to the expense of running a credit card:

1. the interest rate;
2. the length of the interest-free period; and
3. any other charges or benefits.

Which of these is most important to you will depend on how you use your card.

If you always pay off your credit card every month, you're not going to pay interest, so it doesn't matter whether the interest rate is high or low. But you will want to get the maximum interest-free period available, so this is where you will look to distinguish between the cards on offer.

If you find that there are cards that have a similar length before charging interest, then look to see what other charges are attached to the card. Is there an annual fee? Are there high charges on withdrawing money from a cashpoint? Do they overcharge for overseas transactions? It's also worth looking to see what rewards and protection schemes come with cards. Do they provide insurance on goods bought with the card? Are there discounts for cardholders on other services such as utility bills?

But if you look at yourself in the mirror and see someone who isn't really going to keep a clean slate each month, then you'll need to look closely at the interest rates, which are usually shown as the annual percentage rates (APR).

Interest rates

There really is a very large difference between the interest charged by the cheapest cards and the most expensive. There are credit cards charging over 30 per cent APR and there are others which have introductory offers of 0 per cent. And there are cards charging everything in between.

Credit cards

These rates change all the time, but the principle remains the same: you should avoid paying unnecessary interest. As a snapshot of how much the rates vary, in October 2001, here are 10 cards and their interest rates:

- Egg 0 per cent (introductory offer);
- Cahoot 8 per cent;
- Co-operative Platinum 9.8 per cent;
- Nationwide Gold 14.6 per cent;
- Barclaycard 18.9 per cent;
- HSBC 18.9 per cent;
- NatWest 18.9 per cent;
- RSPB donation card 19.8 per cent;
- Lloyds TSB Asset 19.9 per cent;
- Ikea store card 29 per cent.

Rate tarts

This label should be worn as a badge of pride. The 'rate tart' is someone who shifts from card to card looking for the best deal. Why pay 18.9 per cent when you can get six months of interest-free credit? These offers change from month to month and the committed rate tart will follow the low interest deals, ditching cards as they become less competitive.

Whatever type of card you have they all provide more or less the same function. And if you're going to be paying interest, you may as well pay as little as possible. You're never going to get a thank you letter from your lender for all that extra interest you're paying them.

If your card is charging almost 20 per cent APR and you're offered 10 per cent APR elsewhere, it's a very direct saving and you should contact the cheaper company and see if you can transfer the balance and pay a lower rate. *Don't be intimidated* by the idea of swapping your current card for a better offer, because credit companies are fighting for your custom and will make it easy to transfer your outstanding balance. It usually only takes a phone call – and there are few simpler ways of saving yourself money.

If you're trying to pay off a card and have stopped using it for new purchases, then moving to a cheaper rate makes even more sense. If you're paying back a few thousand, then put this onto a cheaper rate card, cut up the old card (so you won't be tempted) and then pay back at a lower rate each month, with the end result that you'll have paid less interest and have cleared your debt more quickly.

If you want an overview of the current best deals, you can either check the personal finance sections of newspapers, which run tables comparing credit card interest rates once a week, or look on a personal finance Web site, such as moneyfacts.co.uk, moneyextra.co.uk, moneysupermarket.co.uk or moneyunlimited.co.uk. Even though the specific offers from credit lenders vary each month, the basic principle of looking for the best rate will continue to apply.

Interest-free periods

If you are a credit card saint and never fall into the trap of paying out interest, then you'll be paying close attention to how long you can go without being charged interest for any purchases on your card.

This can be up to two months, which means that you're getting two months' interest-free credit. You can go on holiday, stack up a load of bills on the card, and then clear it when you come home, without having to pay any interest for the money you've used.

If you're sufficiently organized to be able to keep out of the interest zone, then find a card with the longest interest-free period. These are not advertised as aggressively as low interest rates, but card providers will have to show the interest-free period.

Charges

I've always thought that being asked to pay an annual fee for a credit card was a rip-off – like charging people to go into a supermarket – but there are quite a few cards with an annual charge of between £10 and £20. But there are many more without charges, so don't feel that you have to accept a card that bills you 20 quid before you've even hit the shopping centre.

Another area in which you'll face credit card charges is in withdrawing money from a cashpoint machine, with most cards imposing a 'cash advance' fee. If you do this abroad, many cards also have an overseas transactions charge, which will mean a second bite out of your holiday money.

There is some dispute over the fairness of these charges, which are often rather vaguely described as 'handling fees', but it's worth finding out in advance whether these charges apply to your card. There are cards, such as those offered by Frizzell and Nationwide, which don't charge extra for withdrawals in Europe.

Minimum repayments

All credit cards have a minimum percentage or amount of outstanding debt that you have to repay each month, perhaps 5 per cent of the total owed.

But there has been a recent trend towards lower minimum repayments, which sound as if they're doing the cardholder a favour – 'affordable, low repayments' – which in practice are another wheeze that works to the long-term advantage of the lender. As an example, if you owe £3,000 and pay it back via the minimum repayment of 5 per cent, it'll take nine and half years to clear and cost over £1,000 in interest. But if you pay the same sum back through a monthly minimum of 2 per cent, it'll take 37 years and cost £5,400. Which means more of your money disappearing into interest. So the quicker you pay, the less you pay.

Reward schemes and incentives

Along with low interest rates, interest-free periods and no annual fee, the next item on your credit card checklist is to see if there any other additional goodies that can be thrown in, such as travel insurance, air miles, cashbacks, extended warranties or purchase protection. If you're buying over the Internet, having a credit card that offers purchase protection can be a useful bonus, so check to see the extent of cover offered.

If you're looking for these extra incentives rather than the interest rate, look beyond such vague claims as 'travel insurance included' and make sure you know how much cover is being offered and in what circumstances, because this will vary widely.

And as with any promise of bonuses or freebies, make sure you don't get distracted from the bigger picture. There's no point paying a fortune in interest each year just so you can have a credit card that comes with a free cuddly toy and a discount for an amusement park you're never going to visit.

Credit references: are you worthy?

Before you'll be accepted for a credit card, your credit worthiness will be checked. This will look at factors such as how much you earn, whether you're a homeowner, how much you owe elsewhere and how you've managed credit in the past. If your credit history shows that you've borrowed and paid back without problems, this will improve your credit rating. But if you have a record of unpaid debt or you're already in trouble with other credit cards, don't be surprised if you get rejected. If you feel you've been wrongly put down as a dodgy borrower, then you can pay to see information held about you by credit reference agencies, the two largest of which are Experian and Equifax.

How do credit cards compare to other borrowing?

If you're borrowing hundreds rather than thousands – and you have a low interest card – then credit cards can be one of the cheaper forms of borrowing. Only a few years ago this wouldn't have been the case, with credit cards seen as an expensive way of getting into debt. But there's been strong competition that has pushed down interest rates on credit cards and an overdraft on your current account can now be more expensive. If you're going for larger borrowing, then check out personal loans and you could consider adding the borrowing to your mortgage.

The golden rule is… that there isn't really a golden rule. You have to take charge of your own spending and make sure you're getting a good deal. If you get a good personal loan it's going to be cheaper than a bad credit card. If you get a good credit card it's going to be better than a bad personal loan.

Store cards

It always seems like a tempting offer. You're about to pay for something – maybe clothes or a trolley-load of DIY materials – and the salesperson asks if you'd like to get an immediate discount. All you need to do is to sign up for a store card.

It sounds like an easy saving – but is it a good deal? If you can pay off your store card every month, then you've nothing to lose. But if you're an ordinary human being, and you have a tendency to carry forward a balance on your cards, then you could end up paying some of the highest interest rates on any type of card.

There are 22 million store cards in circulation, a huge number considering the general opinion that many of these cards are a rip-off, charging much more than credit cards, with no obvious benefits over using a conventional credit card or, even better, a debit card. There are exceptions to this. For instance, the John Lewis store card has an interest rate that is lower than many credit cards. So again, check the rate and not the picture on the front.

Debit cards

Debit cards are becoming more and more popular, offering the convenience of credit cards without the risk of building up debt. If you can afford to pay up-front for purchases, the debit card is the cheapest possible option – because there is no interest charged. With a debit card, such as a Switch card, money is deducted directly from a bank account.

As well as being available to use over the counter and on the phone, you can also use some debit cards in cashpoint machines when you're abroad, such as those with the Cirrus badge.

Gold, platinum and loser cards

The more money you have, the less you have to pay, is one of those cruel truths about finance. Gold and platinum cards offer better interest rates than the standard card, and a condition is that cardholders earn above a certain income. It doesn't mean you're rich, but it means you're not poor, and in credit terms, it means you're a lower risk and higher spender.

'Loser card' isn't something that you'll see on advertising, but as the credit card market has grown, so new groups of customers are being targeted, including those who would once have been considered too high a risk. This includes people who have had credit problems or who are on a low income. These cards, reflecting the risk, charge high rates of interest, approaching the levels of store cards. The lenders would argue that they are extending credit to people who would otherwise not be able to get onto the credit ladder. But there have been concerns that this is taking even more interest from people who have the least money and are at risk of getting even deeper into debt.

Card fraud

Fraud has become a major problem for lenders, with the figure of £293 million in 2000, up 55 per cent on the previous year. The biggest increase has been in producing counterfeit cards, known as 'skimming'. This typically involves someone surreptitiously swiping your credit card through a machine that can copy and download its details. This could take place anywhere you hand over your card, such as a restaurant. A fake card is then produced elsewhere, possibly overseas, and the first the victim knows about it is when the statement arrives and it shows you've been on a spending spree in Hong Kong, at a time when you were at home watching television.

To counter fraud, security is set to be increased, with cards protected by a microchip, and instead of using a signature, customers will have to tap in a PIN code number when they're making a purchase.

The current top five forms of card fraud, according to the Association for Payment Clearing Services, are:

1. counterfeit cards;
2. cards stolen or lost;
3. card not present (phone, Internet, post);
4. cards intercepted in the post;
5. fraudulent applications.

Here are the *top tips* for cardholders to guard against fraud from the Association for Payment Clearing Services:

- Guard your cards – never leave them unattended and try not to let them out of your sight while in a shop or restaurant.
- Contact your card issuer immediately if you spot any transactions you don't recognize on your statement.
- Make regular checks to ensure you still have your cards. Report any loss immediately so a stop can be placed on the card.
- Do not discard your receipts – keep them safely and check them off against your statement.
- Never disclose your PIN to anyone.

Donation and supporter cards

A growth area in credit cards has been for organizations such as charities, trade unions and a range of clubs and associations to offer 'affinity' cards, which make a donation every time you make a purchase on the credit card.

The appeal of these cards is that money goes straight to a cause you support, which makes it an easy way to channel money to a charity. But the question to consider is, how much goes to the charity and how much more are you paying in interest?

The typical amount received by charities from these donation credit cards is 0.25 per cent, which means that they receive £1 for every £400 you spend on transactions using the card. But the interest rate charged by these cards tends to be higher than for 'ordinary' cards, so that you might be paying 16 per cent APR rather than 10 per cent APR. Now this extra interest goes to the credit card company, not the charity, so you have to balance whether the extra you're paying in interest is greater than the money that goes to the charity. And if you feel that the credit card company is getting a better deal than the charity, then it might be better to simply donate money directly to the charity and get yourself a better deal on a credit card.

It's also worth making sure that you're not paying more for the sake of a logo or picture on your plastic. Football club credit cards might have a picture of your favourite player, but do you really want to subsidize his wages by paying higher interest rates? Why not just get an ordinary credit card, Sellotape his picture onto it and save yourself the price of a match ticket?

There are also cards with pictures of cats or dogs that are advertised with lines such as, 'Show how much you love dogs by getting our credit card' – which needless to say means that you are getting a dog of a credit card for the sake of a cutesy picture.

What's on the cards for cards?

Credit and debit cards are going to continue to increase in popularity, with studies suggesting that the overwhelming factor for this growth is 'convenience', says Matthew Whittaker, head economist of the Credit Card Research Group. And while credit cards remain the dominant card, debit cards are set to close the gap and will in time overtake credit cards in popularity.

There is an underlying trend towards using cards rather than cash, with younger consumers appearing the most ready to embrace cashless payments. In parts of Europe this process is well advanced, with 86 per cent of transactions in Iceland now being non-cash.

Security is also likely to be tightened up for credit cards, with the introduction of PIN numbers for transactions (rather than signatures) and the use of microchips to monitor usage and to warn against fraud.

Matthew Whittaker also forecasts a shake-out among credit card companies, with competition forcing some cards out of business. And he suggests there might a division between the cards that attract customers with an aggressive pricing policy and other cards that will offer rewards and benefits to a more longstanding customer base.

The psychology of credit card debt

Debt can bring feelings of stress and ill health and can become a great psychological burden, says Dr John Golding, a psychologist at the University of Westminster who has studied the impact of debt.

When people feel under pressure they can act *irrationally* and one of the central features of people under stress is that their attention narrows and they are less able to look beyond their problems to possible solutions. This might mean that someone is so worried about being in debt that they are not able to act in a way that will begin to tackle the problem.

Credit cards are one of the *easiest ways of getting into debt* – you don't have to hand over any money and it pushes the problem of repayment into the future. There are also certain types of people who are vulnerable to getting into debt. These include those who never really think about what they're doing, people who are disengaged from the reality of their own actions, or those who are deceiving themselves about how much they owe. There are also people who show signs of addictive behaviour, appearing to be unable to stop themselves from using credit cards.

Whatever the reasons for getting into debt, the process of putting off payment can lead to an accumulation of anxiety that can restrict your ability to think clearly. You're so worried by the problem that you can't think how to tackle it.

Ten things about credit cards to dazzle your friends

- There are over 1,500 different brands of credit card.
- There are over 100 million credit and debit cards in circulation.
- Credit card spending has increased at an average of 15 per cent per year for five years.
- Debit cards were launched in 1987 and are overtaking credit cards in popularity.
- Credit reference agencies handle 200,000 inquiries per day.
- PIN numbers will soon be required to make a credit card purchase.
- Credit cards were first introduced in the USA in the late 1950s.
- Christmas spending in 2001 put £9.8 billion on debit cards and £8.8 billion on credit cards.
- Credit card fraud cost £293 million in 2000, up 55 per cent on the previous year.
- The largest single source of fraud was counterfeit card use, known as 'skimming' or 'cloning'.

Modern money: credit card junkie

Cathy, aged 32, is a senior manager in a multinational. She's had five cards at a time, running up debts of up to £14,000.

> I suppose you could say that I'm a credit card junkie. When you say how much money I owed it seems so much, but it builds up so slowly and it always seems like something that'll get straightened out on the next statement. It's not a wild weekend, it's months of meals and trips and clothes and… you turn around and then it all starts to sound serious. It starts to sound like debt.
>
> I was beginning to flinch when the post arrived, because the credit card statements had balances that were bigger than my entire take home salary. Without saying anything to anyone about it, I was getting scared of being out of my depth. I started to think that if anything happened, if I lost my job or anything bad happened, then I was going to go straight under.
>
> It was also clear that no one was going to stop me. I'm sure I could have applied for more cards, or a loan to pay off the cards. Every time I reached the limit on a card, it went up another notch.

Earning £38,000 a year, single and living in London, with a £110,000 mortgage, Cathy is used to money coming in and going straight out again. And credit cards were a way of grabbing any passing treat that seemed important at the time.

> It wasn't about borrowing, it was about spending. It was about buying two pairs of shoes, when you couldn't decide which one you wanted most. Or going away for the weekend when you knew you couldn't really afford it. The borrowing was a by-product of the whole shopping trip experience.

Cathy didn't seek any professional advice, but she could see that the repayments were getting out of hand. And so she began a tough love programme of not spending and paying off the cards. Three of the cards were cut up. This budgeting was still only generating enough savings to keep her head above water, so she took out some equity from her house and used that to clear most of the debt. It increased the mortgage, but it meant she had much lower monthly payments.

But even though most of the debt was cleared, she kept two credit cards. Not long afterwards she found herself building up a balance once again, feeling at first a kind of exhilaration that so much credit was available.

> It was a bit like someone saying not to think about drinking orange juice. As soon as they say it, that's what you're thinking about. And I would go out, armed with the cards, telling myself that I didn't need to buy anything, but knowing that I would. I'd then have strange guilt pangs about what I'd bought, but on some level that made it even more enjoyable, as though it was something slightly illicit. Even though the only person who would be paying off the bill would be myself.
>
> I'm not really worried, because it's only a few thousand now. And I know plenty of people who have much bigger balances. But sometimes I look back and I think of all the money I've paid back, and all those interest charges, and it makes me think how much I might have kept for myself. And I suppose I wonder whether it's starting again.

3

Mortgage hunting – the loan rangers

Buying a house is likely to be the biggest purchase of your life. You'll hear that again and again, accompanied by all the usual warnings about making sure you make the right decision in choosing a mortgage and not borrowing too much. But the fact that we agree that this is serious doesn't make the decision any easier. And when we're talking about borrowing over 25 years, how can anyone be sure that they're making the right choice?

> The problem is often too much information rather than too little... And the temptation is to close your eyes and jump.

The problem is often too much information rather than too little, as lenders and advisers bury you in brochures and printouts. And the temptation is to close your eyes and jump – a friend of mine once admitted that he'd spent more time choosing a suit than a mortgage.

Even if you listen to all the advice and spend your lunch hours having the same conversation with dozens of mortgage sellers, you can still end up with the wrong mortgage.

A decade ago, everyone was signing up for endowment mortgages – and if you went into a bank or a building society and talked about the mortgage options, chances are you'd walk out with an endowment. And looking back, there wasn't much chance in it. We were all being sent down endowment alley.

In 1988, 81 per cent of new mortgages were endowments, and the figure remained over 75 per cent for the following three years. I don't remember anyone saying there was an element of risk, nobody was suggesting these mortgages could leave people falling short by tens of thousands of pounds. But now the collective wisdom is that endowment mortgages are Not A Good Thing and there are some lenders that won't even sell them any more.

Without being too gloomy about it, the whole endowment story shows how difficult it is for customers to make a decision about choosing a mortgage. When we signed up for endowments no one had been forced into it, but it's not too difficult to use quotes and initial lower monthly repayments in a way that pushes people in one particular direction. It wasn't a random choice that saw so many people opt for endowments.

And when the wind changed for endowments, the way that homebuyers were steered away from them was just as dramatic. By the beginning of 2001, only 11 per cent of first-time buyers were choosing endowment mortgages, reflecting the changed attitudes towards what had once been the most common type of mortgage. If we come back in another 10 years' time will there be another type of mortgage seen as a bad idea?

So how do we make a sensible decision about getting a good deal that will be secure in the longer term? Without the benefit of seeing into the future, all we can do is to look at everything that's available and which seems most appropriate to our own circumstances.

Before looking at the type of mortgages that are available, it's worth considering a couple of factors that can get forgotten in the whole roller coaster ride of getting a mortgage and moving home.

You are the customer

That might sound obvious. But when you begin looking for mortgages, it's very easy for the relationship to begin to stack up for the lender rather than the borrower. The language of applying for a mortgage is still about the lender agreeing to provide you with a loan, with an unstated suggestion that you should be grateful for what they've given you. There's something of an historical overhang here: in the past it was much more difficult to arrange a mortgage and there was pressure on consumers to fit in with the requirements laid down by banks and building societies.

But today, assuming that you have a decent credit record and you're not seeking to borrow an unrealistically large amount, then you should be aware that *you hold plenty of strong cards.* When a bank or building society offers to lend you money, they're preparing the way for you to pay them thousands of pounds in interest for years to come. You are their profit and they want your custom. So make sure you're getting what you want from them and not what they want from you.

There's a great deal of stress in the whole process of applying for a mortgage and moving home – and with so much going on in the background it's tempting to take what you're given, just in the interests of a quiet life. But with a mortgage you have to live with your decisions for a long time. And it's worth taking the time to step back, think twice, take advice and not be rushed into decisions.

There's something unreal about the amounts of money that come under discussion – and suddenly sticking another £10,000 on the borrowing sounds like small change. But it's still a great big wedge of money – and it's going to be worth as much again in interest over the life of a 25-year mortgage, so don't get sheep-dogged into the first open gate.

The same applies to charges. You are the customer and you're going to be spending a great deal of money, so if they tell you there's a couple of hundred pounds as a fee for something or other that you don't quite understand, ask them to explain and challenge whether it's strictly necessary. And ring round other lenders to see how their charges compare.

A mortgage is going to cost you money: there's no point pretending it won't. But if you make sure you're not overpowered by all the jargon and not scared of asking questions, it's less likely that you'll end up feeling as though you've been fleeced.

Follow the money

This might sound like strange advice, but forget about the place you want to buy. Of course the reason you want a mortgage is to get the keys to your dream house, but all the temptations of thinking about your perfect home can confuse the cold-blooded business of borrowing money.

It's so easy to get pushed along by the conveyor belt of house buying and mortgages. You can be so swept away with the idea of living in this new place that you can forget to put on the handbrake and think about the financial commitments you're about to make.

So, put aside the house, beautiful as it's going to be, and think about the pounds and pence. Think of it as a loan, a straightforward transaction based on what you can sensibly afford. Just follow the money and nothing else. Forget the price tag on the house and think about the price tag on what you're borrowing. Because a mortgage isn't about buying a dream house, it's about borrowing money. And the less you can borrow, and the more you can pay as a deposit, the less you'll have to throw away on interest.

Look at how much it's going to cost in interest payments. After 10 years of a 25-year repayment mortgage you'll probably have paid off about a fifth of the debt which, looked at another way, means that *after 120 monthly payments you'll still owe about 80 per cent of the original sum borrowed.*

For example, if you borrow £100,000 over 25 years on a repayment mortgage, as well as paying back the £100,000 you'll pay back at least another £100,000 in interest, and almost certainly much more. And even if the house price plunges and it's worth much less than you paid for it, you still owe just as much. Because it's the money you've borrowed that matters – and the swings and roundabouts of the housing market won't change the repayments.

Again, it might not seem fair, but the value of your home might go down at the same time that interest rates go up. So be pragmatic and think about how your finances would withstand another couple of percentage points being added to the interest rate. In 2001, interest rates were lowered six times, but they could just as easily have increased six times.

Mortgages are long-term arrangements and you really *don't know what's around the corner* and how much slack you need to allow yourself. Here's a real example: if you'd signed up for a mortgage at the beginning of January 1985, the bank rate stood at 10.5 per cent. By the end of the month, after a couple of increases, the rate was 14 per cent. How would you stand such an upward lurch in monthly repayments?

I promised not to throw around too many charts or graphs, but it's worth looking in detail at the impact of interest rate increases on repayments. If you borrowed £100,000 on a 25-year repayment mortgage, that would cost £591 a month at 5 per cent. But look how the figure rises as interest rates are increased:

£100,000 repayment mortgage at	**Monthly repayments**
5 per cent	£591
6 per cent	£652
7 per cent	£715
8 per cent	£780
9 per cent	£848
10 per cent	£918
11 per cent	£989
12 per cent	£1,062

Again, think about this in the cold light of day, rather than after a bottle of wine when you're thinking about the view from your new windows. If this were a loan for a car or for a holiday, would you borrow right up to the limit, with your home at stake if the interest rates twitch in the wrong direction? It's partly the crazy prices people have to pay for houses, but there is something reckless in the way we stack up debts for buying property. In almost any other context, if someone said they were borrowing a quarter of a million from the bank, you'd think they were insane. But because it's a loan to move house, we think it's normal.

It's always worth remembering that in the second half of the last decade over 200,000 properties were repossessed because of arrears with mortgages.

What are the main types of mortgage on offer?

Repayment

This is the old faithful of mortgages, which despite all the gimmicks and fashions has kept its place as one of the most popular forms of borrowing for a house.

With a repayment mortgage, you agree to pay back a sum of money plus interest over a fixed number of years, with all the debt cleared at the end of the life of the mortgage. Unlike endowments or any stock market-related mortgage, you can be sure that at the end of the agreed repayment period all the debt will be paid.

Repayments come with a number of different features, such as fixed rates and capped rates, but the same basic principle applies. You're agreeing to pay back a loan plus interest, with the debt divided up into monthly payments stretching out over the next 20 or 25 years.

For the first years of a repayment mortgage almost all the payments go into interest, which is a bit depressing when you read your statement and discover after a year of paying thousands of pounds you only owe a hundred quid less than when you started. The capital sum is mostly cleared in the later stages of a repayment mortgage.

If you haven't got a mortgage that sets a limit on interest rate rises, such as a fixed or capped rate, then the amount you pay back each month can change over the life of a mortgage, depending on the ups and downs of interest rates. And once the fixed or capped period ends, then you'll be cast out on the open sea of variable rates. And if rates are rising, then your monthly repayment will also go up. Looking on the brighter side, if interest rates go down, you'll be paying less than you might have expected.

Just because a repayment is the Steady Eddy of mortgages, it doesn't mean that your monthly mortgage payment won't be liable to change.

Fixed rate

The fixed rate is a variation on the repayment theme, which allows you to know for a period of time exactly how much you're going to be paying each month.

Monthly repayments usually rise and fall with interest rates, but a fixed rate mortgage provides a guaranteed interest rate for the duration of the arrangement – which is going to be something like the first two or three years of a mortgage, after which the repayment will revert to the variable rate.

The benefit of this type of mortgage is that *borrowers know exactly how much they're going to have to pay* and so can budget accordingly, with no fears of a sudden hike in interest payments. If interest rates rise above the level of the fixed rates, then people with this type of mortgage can feel suitably smug. But if rates fall, they're going to be fixed at a rate higher than everyone else is paying.

There is no magic formula for knowing whether a fixed rate is going to work in the borrower's favour, so its strongest selling point is as a promise of stability and predictability in terms of monthly outgoings.

If you're considering a fixed rate, check if there are any kind of tie-ins or penalties to keep you after the fixed rate finishes.

Capped

This is a further refinement of the fixed rate, which sets an upper limit on interest rates for an agreed number of years. This means that if the variable rate climbs up the graph paper, borrowers with capped mortgages can be protected, knowing they won't have to pay more. The extra benefit is that if interest rates go down, people with capped mortgages can still take advantage of this and will have lower repayments.

This might sound like a win-win for the borrower. But remember that these are all promotional offers, giving you a short-term incentive to sign up. These benefits are only for the opening years of a mortgage and there is plenty of time for lenders to make back anything they lose.

Also, the rates offered for a capped mortgage will not necessarily be the keenest rates available, because as you might have gathered, banks and building societies are not in the habit of giving away money.

Endowment

A decade ago three-quarters of new mortgages were endowments, but now these come with a health warning, and have fallen out of favour because of what is seen as an unacceptably high level of risk. With an endowment mortgage you only pay off the interest each month, and then make a second payment into the endowment – an investment that at the end of the life of the mortgage should have grown enough to pay off the debt.

If the endowment has grown larger than the sum you've borrowed, there could be a bonus at the end of the mortgage. But if the endowment does not grow to meet the amount you've borrowed, you could end up still owing money after 25 years of payments.

Disputes over how these were sold and whether people were made aware of the potential risks are likely to rumble on for years. And the suspicions raised about endowments are likely to cast a cloud over other types of stock market-related mortgages.

The rise and fall of endowments is also a useful warning that economic climates can change and you should not make any assumptions about interest rates and the housing market. Endowments became popular in the years when stock markets appeared to be on a relentless increase and when house prices seemed set to climb forever. But after a protracted house price depression and then faltering stock markets, the endowment bandwagon now looks rather ragged.

Discount

With any of these mortgages there might be a discount on

offer, which usually means a reduced rate of interest for a number of years. It's worth asking what discounts are available, because it might make quite a saving.

But remember that while this can make the mortgage seem more affordable in the short term, make sure that you can budget for the full repayments at the end of the discount. As with all such special offers, it's there to attract customers, with short-term incentives intended to win long-term profits.

Cashback

As the name implies, the incentive is that you get a sum of cash at the beginning of the mortgage. This is usually a percentage of whatever you've borrowed, giving you a few extra thousand to help with furnishing your new home.

The advantage of this is that it gives you some money when you most need it, helping you after you've spent everything on moving house. The disadvantage is that it might mean your payments are set at a higher rate of interest and that you might have to pay back the cashback if you move within a fixed number of years after beginning the mortgage.

Flexible

This term has come to describe a number of different types of mortgage, but the general principle is to make better use of your cash and to make mortgage repayments less rigid.

This can mean allowing borrowers greater control of the speed at which they pay off a mortgage, letting them take repayment 'holidays' and also helping borrowers save money by being able to pay the mortgage off sooner without any penalties. Even if you only over-pay by a small amount each month, it can have a big impact on the total sum you pay to the bank or building society.

There are also flexible mortgages, which are becoming increasingly popular, that allow borrowers to link a mortgage with a bank account, with any credit in the account helping to lower the balance of the mortgage. This cuts down interest – and these mortgages can mean a substantial saving.

With accounts linked to mortgages you don't have to do any of the money shuffling yourself: it should all happen automatically. But it does mean that in the parts of the month when the account is looking healthy (ie just after payday) any spare money is going to be working, rather than just kipping in the bank. And even this passive form of flexible banking is likely to save customers thousands of pounds over the life of the mortgage.

Remortgaging and additional lending

The banks and building societies are competing fiercely for customers and if you already have a mortgage you might be able to find a better offer from another company. There are special offers available from most major lenders designed to entice customers to transfer their mortgages, with the promise of reduced rates of interest and cashbacks.

It has also become much easier to swap mortgage companies, with many lenders offering to pay legal costs and surveys so that there will be little or no charge to switch your mortgage. However, you need to check that your mortgage does not have a clause that would mean that you have to pay a penalty if you move to another lender.

How much can you borrow?

This varies between lenders – and you can negotiate if you think there are special circumstances – but typically banks and building societies will lend three times the amount of a single salary and two and half times a joint income where a couple are buying a home together. But such rules seem to be waived when house prices demand bigger loans. There have been stories in London of lenders offering four and five times salaries, when people can demonstrate they have enough spare income, maybe in the form of bonuses, to meet the repayments.

It shouldn't just be a case of borrowing as much as possible – and just because banks are willing to lend a fortune, it doesn't mean that paying it back will be any easier. If interest rates go up, you need to be confident that you will be able to afford the increase.

If the amount you need to borrow begins to sound like it's crazily high, it might be worth considering buying somewhere cheaper. And one of the handiest ways of gauging prices in local property markets is to check with the Land Registry's Web site (www.landreg.gov.uk), which has stacks of statistics on property prices.

What happens if you can't keep up repayments?

In the last half of the 1990s, over 200,000 homes were repossessed as lenders took back properties on which borrowers had fallen behind with repayments. This can happen for many reasons – redundancy, sickness, divorce – but it is always worth remembering that repayments are linked to the interest rate and that it can rise as well as fall. And if it rises, borrowers need to have enough spare cash to cope with the extra monthly payments. You might also consider insurance offers to protect against financial problems caused by losing a job or ill health.

If you begin to fall behind with payments, it's worth contacting the lender at an early stage, so that the problem can be tackled and arrangements can be made for rescheduling debts. Free advice is available from your local Citizens Advice Bureau.

History lesson: how interest rates can change

This list of bank rates, based on a sample of major high street lenders, shows how much interest rates can change over the course of a mortgage. In the 1990s and in the early part of this decade, we've become accustomed to relatively low interest rates. But in comparison, in the 1980s, the rates were often substantially above 10 per cent:

1980 July	16 per cent
1981 March	12 per cent
1982 January	14 per cent
1983 January	11 per cent
1984 May	9 per cent
1985 January	14 per cent
1986 January	12.5 per cent
1987 March	10.5 per cent
1988 March	9 per cent
1989 May	14 per cent
1990 October	14 per cent
1991 February	13.5 per cent
1992 May	10 per cent
1993 January	6 per cent
1994 February	5.25 per cent
1995 February	6.75 per cent
1996 January	6.25 per cent
1997 May	6.25 per cent
1998 June	7.5 per cent
1999 January	6 per cent
2000 January	5.75 per cent
2001 February	5.75 per cent

Information on the Internet

The leading banks all have their own Internet sites, which can be a useful way of comparing the current offers and interest rates. These can include 'mortgage calculators' which allow you to see how much you can borrow and how much you would have to pay back.

A really useful mortgage calculator is on the Web site of the Council for Mortgage Lenders (www.cml.org.uk). This allows you to compare how much repayments are changed by rises and falls in interest rates. You can put in the sum you want to borrow and frighten yourself by seeing how much you'd pay each month if interest rates doubled overnight.

Another useful online information source is the Land Registry's Web site (www.landreg.gov.uk). This contains a local breakdown of house sales and average prices. When you're looking for a house, you depend so much on anecdotal evidence and what estate agents tell you, and this Web site is a great way of getting some hard facts about the level of house prices wherever you're looking.

What questions should you ask?

The government has suggested a list of the top ten questions that you need to consider when looking for a mortgage:

1. How much can I afford to borrow?
2. How can I tell which mortgage rate is best for me?
3. What is the most appropriate type of mortgage for me?
4. How should I repay it?
5. Can I make lump sum payments to reduce the size of the loan?
6. Are there any redemption penalties?
7. Does this mortgage come with compulsory insurance?
8. What other charges will I have to pay?
9. What happens if I can't pay?
10. What about the small print?

Ten things about mortgages to dazzle your friends

- In August 2001, mortgages worth £16 billion were sold.

- A third of mortgages issued were re-mortgages.

- First-time borrowers' average mortgage was £70,000.

- The average first-time borrowers' mortgage was 2.36 times salary.

- Mortgages represent 81 per cent of all consumer borrowing.

- There are over 11 million mortgages being repaid.

- In 1991, over 75,000 homes were repossessed.

- In 1988, 81 per cent of mortgages sold were endowments.

- The average price in 2001 for a detached house in Kingston-upon-Hull was £78,000; in Kingston-upon-Thames it was £458,000.

- In Greater London in 2001, an average terraced house cost £196,000; in 1996 it was £93,000.

Modern money: sandwiches and interest rates

Simon, aged 29, works as a designer, and signed up for a first mortgage last year.

> Everyone says to shop around, to make sure you do plenty of research. But in the end it came down to meeting my girlfriend at lunchtime and having these rushed conversations with the various banks. There was nothing very organized about it.
> I'd grab a sandwich, and looking back I think I had more informed opinions about choosing the sandwich, and it might even have taken longer to decide which sandwich, than the actual business of choosing a mortgage.
> We'd meet up and go to a series of appointments with all the obvious big name lenders, and it always seemed to involve little cubicles and an adviser with an over-active printer. They would ask loads of questions, filling in all these boxes on their computer screens, and then they'd come back with a few quotes, and reams and reams of paper.
> You couldn't say that you weren't being given information – and you had an opportunity to ask any questions. But looking back, we must have been sitting there like we'd lost the power of speech. You're rushed, you don't really understand the language, and you don't want to sound stupid. And we'd end up saying things like 'maybe we should choose such and such a mortgage because the woman at that bank was friendlier than the others'. As if we were ever going to see her again.
> In the end, it wasn't so much a decision as reaching an indecision. We really didn't know – and we went for one of the cheapest monthly repayments, but it was also because in some non-scientific way this bank seemed more reassuring. I think it was something to do with the colour of the carpets.

4

Savings – think of it as reverse borrowing

I have to admit that spending comes more easily to me than saving. And over the years I've found borrowing a more familiar way of fundraising than saving. I don't think I'm unusual in this, because we live in the land of debt and fast-food finance where credit is easier and quicker than the long-term virtues of saving.

There have been many surveys warning that few of us have enough money put away, with the national 'savings gap' standing at an estimated £27 billion. This is the money that financial experts think we should have put in reserve for a rainy day, but have so far failed to save. While personal finance buffs will say that we should all have at least three months' money put away for an emergency, in practice the most typical level of cash available is about £750 per household and it's claimed that between about a quarter and a third of the population have *little or no savings* at all.

So it seems as though we're lousy at saving. There are a number of reasons that might explain this. Interest rates have been relatively low, which makes saving less attractive. And

> Perhaps we should look at savings as *borrowing in reverse*, because we don't seem to have any difficulties with loans... we're very good at borrowing. So if we could apply our borrowing skills, we'd be onto a winner.

perhaps more importantly, there's been a cultural change in how we see debt. A generation ago there was still a resistance to getting into debt and loans were less easily obtained. But now we borrow first and ask questions later – and spending sprees are much more likely to be funded by credit cards or personal loans than by savings.

But we should have savings. Not least because at the end of the year it's depressing to look at your bank account and to think you've worked for all those days and months and you've nothing to show for it except more debts. This can feel particularly depressing as you march into your 30s and 40s. You have a marriage, mortgage and children, and nothing in the bank except a list of direct debits sucking money out of the account.

The question is, how do we begin to save when there's so little money left after all the loan repayments? And that is a substantial problem, because our personal finances today are often shaped around repaying loans rather than saving for ourselves.

Perhaps we should look at savings as *borrowing in reverse*, because we don't seem to have any difficulties with loans. In fact, we're very good at borrowing. So if we could apply our borrowing skills, we'd be onto a winner. Somehow we manage to raise the money each month to pay off loans, so if we thought about regular savings as the same as paying off debts, but with interest coming in rather than going out, we might begin to see money accumulating rather than disappearing. But that depends on having enough spare cash to begin setting aside.

How can we do that? If you look at your mortgage, personal loans, credit card, fuel and telephone providers, there are almost certainly cheaper alternatives. It's quite possible that you could save £50 to £100 a month just by looking hard for the most cost-efficient options. Changing your mortgage and credit card alone could free up a surprising amount of cash each month.

This *financial MOT* is going to take a few days, looking through the best buys suggested in the personal finance pages of newspapers and seeing where you can make savings, but the end result should be to produce money you didn't know you had. This is money going out that could be coming in. You could use this money to further cut down on debt repayments. But it might be worth beginning to save money, building a reserve, so that the next time you need money you could draw on your savings rather than borrowing even more.

The interest you'll earn in savings is quite possibly, but not necessarily, going to be less than you're paying on your debts. But once you establish the principle of saving there could be much larger long-term advantages. Because it's not until you begin to build up savings that you really can take control of your own finances and can put into practice all those clichés about getting your money working.

When you're in borrowing mode, you're always playing catch-up, following the repayments schedule and pouring all your money into covering loans. When you have savings you can begin to make decisions about how you want to use your money and how it can earn you more.

Savings are like reverse borrowing in other ways. There is a range of short-term and long-term options, with different forms of saving appropriate to different needs. In the classic model of savings, there would be cash immediately available for emergencies, then something locked away in a high interest account and some longer-term money in investments such as unit trusts. But there's no need to follow any kind of convention, as long as you can begin to reap the benefits of earning interest rather than a lifetime of paying it to lenders.

Just as the interest rates for borrowing can no longer be divided into neat categories, the traditional ideas of what types of saving pay the most interest can no longer be relied upon. There are current accounts that pay higher interest than deposit accounts and, when markets are depressed, an investment such as a stocks and share ISA might be earning less than both a deposit and a current account.

As with borrowing, pay attention to the interest rate rather than the label, because there are very wide variations in what savings accounts of all varieties will offer – and if you've made the mighty leap forward and can begin to save, then you'll want to get the greatest benefit.

So ignore the brands and look what's inside. Just because a savings account is called Instant Riches or Midas on a Stick, it doesn't mean that anyone's giving away any favours. And you still need to look at the basic ingredients of interest rates, level of risk and how much notice you need to withdraw money.

The underlying trend among savings accounts is towards greater mobility of money, greater flexibility and fewer rules as to how you can or can't move your money around. The emergence of Internet banks a few years ago has made a considerable and positive impact on what you might get from bank accounts. And the rates of interest you can find with Internet current accounts can hold their own with savings accounts. Such secure savings accounts and cash ISAs have become more popular as the stock markets have been making rather nervous progress and failing to fatten up investments.

If this book had been written a couple of years ago, the mood of the time would have been to ride the upward tide of the markets. But after more sober revisions of potential gains, it's worth remembering that there is never any guarantee of easy money and that there is no quick fix to turn a small amount of money into a big amount of money.

Types of saving

As with most aspects of personal finance, the language of savings and investments seems to have been designed to make sure that nobody understands what anything means. And this mystification throws a fog over what is really a straightforward set of decisions about how you want to save. The three big questions for savings concern how much interest is on offer, the length of notice for withdrawals and the extent of any risk to your money.

There's no perfect choice, it's just a question of finding a compromise that isn't too bad. And in this respect you could almost think of savings as a balancing act between advantages and disadvantages – and you have to pick out the balance that will benefit you most.

In terms of the advantages, you'll want:

- high interest rates;
- instant access;
- no risk;
- no minimum amount to open an account;
- flexibility with payments.

But you'll have to balance this against:

- the notice required to withdraw money;
- limits on how much and how often money can be withdrawn;
- the risk of investments losing value;
- the minimum amounts for opening an account.

What we all want is to have as many of the advantages with as few of the disadvantages as possible. And the banks and building societies want something similar for themselves. It's a matter of meeting somewhere in the middle.

So it usually means a trade-off. If you want to be able to take out your money immediately, you're going to have a lower rate of interest than if you agree to leave the money alone for a couple of years. If you have a great big lump sum and you're willing to leave it in the bank for five years, you'll get an even better rate of interest. And so on.

Levels of risk with savings

- Very low and low risk: current and deposit accounts, savings accounts, cash ISAs, bonds, gilts.
- Medium risk: unit trusts, investment trusts, OEICs (open-ended investment companies).
- Higher risk: shares in riskier markets.

Deposit and savings accounts

Each bank has its own brand names for its savings schemes, but these are usually divided up in terms of how quickly you might need to take out your money and how big a sum you want to invest.

Instant access saver accounts are designed to offer interest while allowing customers to withdraw their money immediately, without any penalties. They often have cashpoint and debit cards to make it easier to get at your money.

These types of accounts have been used traditionally as a kind of halfway house between a current account and longer-term savings, useful for holding fairly modest amounts for the short term. They can usually be opened with a small sum of money, maybe just a pound.

As with credit cards and loans, interest rates vary between banks, so shop around for the best rates available. These change from month to month, so park your money where it's to your greatest benefit.

Notice accounts are intended for money that won't be needed in the short term – and because the money won't be withdrawn immediately, it can earn a higher rate of interest. These might be useful if you had a lump sum that you didn't need for a while, but you still wanted to earn you some cash.

There will be a wide variety of these available, with different rates of interest based around how long you will leave the money untouched. There are accounts which let you withdraw money once a quarter and there are others that require one month or three months' notice before you can take out any money. The longer you agree to tie up your money, the higher the interest.

These types of account will also have thresholds for how much you'll need as a lump sum. If you take the example of the NatWest, you need £2,000 for its 'Diamond Reserve' account, which requires a month's notice for withdrawals. For the three-month notice 'Crown Reserve' account you'll need £50,000, and it allows you to withdraw £250 a month without losing interest.

Internet banks

These newcomers on the banking scene offer very competitive rates of interest, and often appear in the lists of best interest rates available.

Internet banks can offer above-average interest rates for two main reasons – they are much cheaper to run than traditional high street banks; and as new banks, they need to offer attractive rates to build up custom.

There are some people who believe that the rates offered by Internet banks are unsustainably high and, like any promotional offer, will be withdrawn once it has served the purpose of drumming up extra trade. But this longer-term view shouldn't stop anyone from taking advantage of what's on offer at present.

National Savings

National Savings, available in a Post Office near you, offer a range of very safe government-backed saving schemes. These are deposit-style accounts, rather than speculative investments, with savings schemes that include notice accounts, a mini-cash ISA and bonds which pay out a guaranteed monthly income.

This is also the home of the Premium Bond, a mix of lottery and saving that would be considered highly innovative if someone dreamt it up now. But if you think that they belong to an earlier black and white era, it's worth remembering that almost a quarter of a million investors have the maximum £20,000 in Premium Bonds.

Although not the most glamorous way of saving, National Savings say that 30 million people invest with them, with combined savings of £62 billion, making them one of the most widely used ways of saving money.

Children's accounts

These can be divided into two main groups: the accounts which children themselves are going to use and those that are ways in which adults can invest on behalf of children.

Most banks will have junior saver type accounts, which are customized for children, with information and pass books designed to help children get used to the idea of money and savings.

For parents and grandparents wanting to put some money aside for children, there are a number of investment schemes. These assume that the money will be left alone for a number of years, and offer a decent return on the investment. There are 'baby bonds' and 'children's bonds' which provide parents with a fixed rate of interest. And there are other stock-related investments that are targeted at parents. But there are sceptics who say that 'packaged' investments for children can often come with higher charges than a straightforward investment in unit trusts.

Stakeholder pensions have been used by some parents and grandparents as a way of building up funds for children. Paying in money on behalf of a young person when they are at school can generate a considerable amount of money. If you put £300 a month into a stakeholder pension for a child's first 18 years – and then put nothing in again – this will grow to be worth around £840,000 by the time the child is aged 50, which works out at £75,000 per year for the rest of their life (the value of which would depend on inflation in the intervening years).

Individual savings accounts (ISAs)

When ISAs were introduced by the government they were intended to be a simple and popular way to encourage people to save money, with the big incentive that they were tax free. They have been popular but they have never been simple and I wonder how many people who own ISAs understand how they work.

Perhaps what contributes to the confusion is that the ISA seems to mean so many different things. It can be a savings account, a bit of dabbling in shares and it can have something to do with life assurance. And there are maxis and minis and ISA-wrappers and it all seems like it's been designed by people who spend too long playing with their pocket calculators.

But as a ray of light, maybe we should just think of the ISA as a kind of tax break for savers. There are all kinds of accounts and investments flying under the flag of an ISA, but what they all have in common is that they're tax-free. And because this is a tax break, there are limits on how much you can save.

In brief, *a mini-ISA* allows you to put up to £3,000 a year into cash, £3,000 into stocks and shares and £1,000 in life assurance. You can have all three within a year, but if you have a mini-ISA, you can't have a maxi-ISA as well.

A *maxi-ISA* lets you invest up to £7,000 a year and can be made up of a mixture of cash, stocks and shares and life assurance.

This is all at risk of descending into money jargon, but if you choose a maxi- or mini-ISA you'll still need to decide whether you want to put your money into a savings account or into investments linked to the stock market.

The *cash-ISA* is most like a straightforward savings account, with no risk of losing your money and a tax-free rate of interest that might well be above what you'd earn on a regular instance access account. Cash-ISA accounts, which will have all kinds of brand names, will have many of the features of an instant access account, including a small sum to open the account, a cashpoint card and no penalty for withdrawing money.

Stocks and shares ISAs

Whenever anyone mentions investing in stocks and shares, this is accompanied by the warning in fiery letters in the sky that share prices can go down as well as up. The other piece of advice you'll hear is that these are investments for the medium to long term and not for someone who wants a return in a couple of years.

So, health warning out the way, stocks and shares ISAs operate as a way of investing in, you've guessed it, stocks and shares – but without paying any tax. And it's generally agreed that, looking at an overview of past decades, in the long run the best returns for savers are from the stock market.

Stocks and shares ISAs can either be investments in a company or trust you've chosen yourself – which might go under the name of a *self-select share ISA*. Or else it might be an investment scheme in which the shares are selected and managed by a bank or investment company.

Among the most common forms of investment under the ISA tax umbrella will be *unit trusts* – and most of the big banks will have their own versions of unit-trust investments which fall into the category of a stocks and shares ISA.

When you buy into a unit trust, you're buying into a large pool of money invested by many people and organizations, which collectively buys shares and bonds. This spread of investments and the large size of these combined funds should help them to ride out the ups and downs of the stock market and are seen to be safer than piling all the money into a single company or a narrow range of shares.

With unit trusts you can pay in relatively small monthly amounts, perhaps £50, and gradually build up an investment, which should grow over the years. On the downside, there are charges attached to unit trusts, which will chew away at whatever you put in, so when looking at the various unit trust offers consider charges as well as performance.

Investment trusts and open-ended investment companies (OEICs)

These are both ways of buying into pooled investments, in which you add your money to other people's, and the combined amount is re-invested on the stock market, with the aim of generating some extra value.

Unlike unit trusts, the investment trust is not open-ended, but has a fixed number of shares. You buy shares in an investment trust – and it buys shares in other companies. OEICs are distinguished by having a single price for both buying and selling, rather than having different rates for buyers and sellers.

Picking an ISA

As the financial year ends, investment companies will be gearing up with adverts for stocks and shares ISAs, with all kinds of claims about the prowess of their funds. Financial regulators are always keen to make the point that past performance is not necessarily any guide to future levels of growth. So how can we pick an ISA?

The Financial Services Authority suggests a few questions to ask yourself to narrow down the ISA options:

- How much can you afford to invest?
- How long can you afford to have your money tied up? If only for the short term, then consider a cash ISA. For the longer term you could consider a stocks and shares or insurance ISA.
- What are the fees involved in the running of the ISA?
- What is the level of risk you are prepared to take?
- Do you want a mini- or maxi-ISA?

There is also a benchmarking scheme for ISAs, called the 'Cat standard', which is intended to ensure consumers reasonable terms. This kite-marking standard represents: Charges, easy Access and Terms.

Online trading

A couple of years ago, it was difficult to get into a taxi without hearing about how much the driver had made by dealing in shares on the Internet the night before. The spread of the Internet had made desktop share dealing a simple enough process – and the dot com boom had given the impression that you could log on to your computer and help yourself to some juicy profits.

That all seems so long ago – as the crash in technology shares dramatically illustrated the old maxim that share prices can go down as well as up. Plenty of people who were dabbling in shares found themselves losing much of their investments.

But Internet share trading had widened the range of people who played the markets. People who would never have crossed the doorstep of a traditional stockbrokers found themselves buying and selling shares, using the online share services provided by the banks and other specialists.

There is nothing particularly technically difficult about this. If you can handle getting your groceries online, then you'd be able to follow the steps needed to buy and sell shares on the Internet. But what you'll need most of all is money. And not just money you have, but money you don't need to have, money you can afford to lose. If you're going to need this money in a hurry for something like paying the mortgage, it's not the best idea to be using it for a flutter on the stock market. Unlike a flutter on the horses, 'winning' on a share is usually a long-term process. And if the value of your investments goes down for a while, you might find your money tied up for the foreseeable future.

The Internet share-trading boom, like the expansion of share ownership during the privatizations of the 1980s and 1990s, made people feel as though they could come inside the magic circle of share dealing. They were running alongside the big wheels of Wall Street and the City. But if you take a step back, the big money is still being made by the big money, because if you're investing huge sums you can make huge sums with only a slight change in share prices. If you're sticking on a couple of hundred quid, your gains are going to be as modest as the investment. You might make more than you'd ever get from sticking it in the bank, but it's not going to generate enough money to change your life.

If you think of it in terms of gambling on horses, the size of the win is going to be affected by the odds – but even more by the size of the stake. And with online trading, there is another disincentive in that each time you trade a share you have to pay a charge of perhaps £10 or £12.

That isn't to say that online trading is a good or a bad thing. In many ways it is a democratizing force that you can turn on your computer and enter the stock market. But it's not a magic money maker and the minnows in the market are always at risk of being swallowed up by the big fishes.

Ethical finance

There are a growing number of financial products designed to address consumers' ethical concerns about how money is invested.

If you're putting money into any kind of savings scheme, whether it's into an ISA or a pension, there are usually ethical alternatives that are designed to screen out investing in companies which might be associated with environmental damage, human rights abuse or cruelty to animals.

Ethical finance might once have been considered a niche market, but it is steadily moving into the mainstream, and many of the larger companies will be offering ethical options as part of their selection of investment routes. Any financial adviser should be able to point your money towards an ethical investment fund.

This growth in ethical awareness among finance companies also reflects demand from consumers. The Co-operative Bank, which has a longstanding ethical investment policy, says that its ethical stance has been one of the main reasons that customers choose it rather than another bank.

Clear your debts before saving?

If you owe money, is it better to clear all your debts before starting to save?

As with many questions about money, this depends on the type of person you are and how well you know yourself. In theory it makes more sense to clear credit cards and personal loans first – and then when you're back on the straight and narrow, it might be time to start saving.

The reason for this would be that interest rates on credit cards and loans are likely to be higher than the interest you're earning on savings, so whatever you make in interest on savings, you're losing more on what you owe. Therefore, the logic of this argument is that you concentrate on cutting out paying interest on debts.

But human nature doesn't work like a calculator. And I must admit that scrapping savings and focusing on clearing debts might mean, in my rather disorganized case, that I would end up not quite clearing all my debts and having no savings either.

With credit cards, there's a great temptation just to let the balance rise up again, so you never quite stamp out the last few pounds of debt. And the longer that takes, the longer you would miss out on savings.

So even if it doesn't make complete financial sense, it might make better psychological sense to keep putting something aside, as well as chipping away at the credit cards and personal loans.

Ten things about savings that will dazzle your friends

- Typical household savings are £750.
- Over a quarter of households have no savings.
- The recommended minimum savings is three months' salary.
- Only a third of adults are making provision for retirement.
- In the year ending April 2001, £29.8 billion was invested in ISAs.
- In the year ending April 2001, 11 million ISA accounts were opened.
- Cash mini-ISAs are the most popular form of ISA.
- Seven and a half million people access bank accounts online.
- In 1973 the first female members were admitted to the London Stock Exchange.
- You can win £1 million on Premium Bonds.

Modern money: savings? Maybe next year

Graham is 38, with a 5-year-old son, and is separated from his former partner. He works in local government and earns £28,000 a year. Even though he has worked for the past 17 years, he has so far never saved any money. Each month, the current account dips down until it's almost empty, and is then re-charged by his salary. Almost as soon as payday has passed, a series of standing orders, the mortgage and deductions reduce the balance, so that there is only a residual amount left for spending money. This is often topped up by credit cards or an overdraft.

All this worries Graham, because every month seems to follow the same pattern of edging slightly deeper into debt. It's not a debt problem, but there's no sign of beginning to make savings. This is not unusual now, for white-collar graduate workers to be living without any financial padding. And what keeps them in a plentiful supply of white collars is often easy credit, rather than savings.

On a good day, he thinks that he earns enough not to worry about the rate at which his money disappears without touching the sides. But on a bad day, he thinks that he is very vulnerable to any loss of income, and it means that he is trapped in his job forever. And he also reflects that he had more spending power when he was just starting work than he has now.

He is also aggrieved that even if he wanted to start saving, the little he can get together is ridiculously small compared with what he needs. After separating, he and his former partner sold their shared house, and he now has a mortgage on a flat. He'd like to move, but anything he likes is far out of his financial reach. He says that in his parents' day, people saved up before looking for a house. But now trying to save is pointless, when house prices can increase by thousands in a couple of weeks. Saving becomes a waste of time for house hunters, he says, because savings can never keep up with the sky-high property prices.

Next year, he plans to begin putting money aside. Honestly.

5

Pensions – when will I see you again?

Pensions are complicated and depressing

Even the sound of the word 'pensions' is depressing. And when you look more closely it doesn't get any better, because you soon find they're expensive, complicated and they only pay off after years of investment. But like many uncomfortable and unpleasant things, they're also very important.

There's something about money that says 'Spend Me', in six-foot high letters. But what pensions are saying is 'Don't Spend Me', instead give it to some guy in a suit, and with a bit of luck, in another 30 years or so, another guy in a suit will give it back.

It isn't exactly a sales pitch that's going to win over the instant gratification generation. But people who are now in their 20s, 30s and 40s are the ones who are most likely to need to make their own pension provision, because all the signs suggest that when we retire, the state pension will be worth very little. Even if it manages to stay the equivalent of today's state pension, how would you feel about living for 20 years of retirement on less than £300 a month?

> Only about a third of adults have a pension, other than the state pension. ... one of the most reassuring financial conversations I've ever had was with a pensions expert of many years who admitted that he still found it difficult to understand how many pensions worked.

Fear and loathing in my bank account

The increase in the state pension a couple of years ago of 75 pence a week should have given a clue to the long-term fate of the state pension. And in true Treasury style, when a pensioner sent back a cheque for 75 pence as a protest, the cheque was promptly lodged.

But the fact that most people know the state pension won't be much use still hasn't persuaded enough people to set up their own pension. If you're in a job that has a pension scheme, then you're in a better position, but there are many people who don't have access to work pensions, and they are facing a bleak retirement.

Only about a third of adults have a pension, other than the state pension. And this figure is even lower for women, with only 27 per cent reported to have their own pension. Only two fifths of people in work have pensions.

So concerned has the government been about the lack of pension provision that it has created a new type of pension – *the stakeholder* – which is designed to be flexible and affordable and is specifically intended for those people who don't have occupational pensions. It aims to bring pensions within the reach of people on lower incomes who often don't have work schemes, people who are part-time or contract workers, the self-employed and mothers who take time out of work to bring up families.

Stakeholders have been pitched as being a square deal, a more wholesome kind of savings plan, which will reassure the public that they're getting value for money. This isn't accidental, because the pensions industry has been blighted by an image problem. It's not what you read in the pensions brochures, but people have been wary of the whole concept of private pensions, fearing that this was more about spivvery and salesmen's commissions than making a sound provision for retirement.

Private pensions were seen as a Thatcherite experiment, associated with a git in a suit with a briefcase and a quick getaway lined up if things went pear shaped. Of course this was unfair to the majority of honest pension sellers, but there has been a sense in which people haven't quite trusted the idea of a private pension.

The publicity surrounding pensions mis-selling in the late 1980s and early 1990s can't have helped matters. This involved the selling of private pensions to people who already had better occupational pensions, so that they were opting out of decent pension schemes for a private version that was more expensive and was likely to give lower returns.

While work-based pensions, with the security and support of an employer, are widely seen as A Good Thing, the freestanding private pension has failed to win the hearts and minds of the public. And it still remains to be seen whether stakeholder pensions will be different enough to reach the parts that other pensions have not reached.

Within the more affluent end of the self-employed market – businessmen rather than window cleaners – private pensions are well established and there is a relatively high take-up. And among people who have access to work-based pensions, there is a high take-up. But that leaves a great number of people outside these groups, but who will still need an income in retirement. And this middle ground is the real challenge for stakeholder pensions.

Pensions are also notoriously *complicated*. And one of the most reassuring financial conversations I've ever had was with a pensions expert of many years who admitted that he still found it difficult to understand how many pensions worked. So we should be honest and say they are complicated – and it has never helped that they are sold in a way that does little to make them more comprehensible.

When you start looking at the jaw-breaking jargon, it's all too easy to switch off and stop trying to make sense of what's being offered. And even though pensions companies will spend a fortune in promoting their wares (usually with pictures of perfect families looking perfectly smug) they've done little to put their products in reach of the English language.

Cast your eye over any pensions literature and you'll start bumping into phrases such as 'with-profits annuity', 'actively managed funds', 'money purchase', 'AVCs',

'FSAVCs', 'actuarially reduced benefits' and all the rest of it. You can find out what all these terms mean, but should we really have to approach a pension like code breakers trying to find out what the enemy are talking about? And if you don't understand something, that's when mistakes are most easily made.

Maybe pensions shouldn't be called pensions

This isn't entirely flippant, as there have been suggestions that the term isn't consumer-friendly enough. Or else that it makes us think of queues at the Post Office and something being handed out by the government.

When we're talking about a pension, we're really talking about another long-term investment, with a few more tax breaks. What you put in will determine how much you take out. There isn't anything particularly fair about this, but money isn't always fair – and if you're rich and can afford to stuff money into a pension, it's going to mean you have more when you retire.

Once you strip away all the jargon, a pension means investing a load of money now, either as a lump sum, monthly payments or both, which will grow over the years – and whatever it makes in that time will be the money you have to keep you in retirement.

Often when you see pension plans these pots of money sound huge – but think of it in terms of how much money you might need to keep you for 30 years. If you lost your job tomorrow, how much money would you need to keep going for the rest of the year? And if you were never going to work again, *how much would you need for the rest of your life?*

This means we'll all need to have enough money put away for a decent pension. That's easy enough to say. But it's not easy choosing a pension. How do we know that we're not chucking the pensions money down a black hole every month?

It's difficult choosing something that is so difficult to imagine. It's like trying to choose curtains over the phone. We want to feel and see what we're buying, but all we get are forecasts. We won't really know what the pension will be like until we start collecting it, years from now, by which point any problems will be hard to resolve. And this leaves us with an ingrained fear that we might be putting money into something that will turn out to be a disappointment when we need it.

But given that we do need to have something invested for when we retire, what are the types of decisions we'll need to make?

Company pensions

If you work for a company that offers a pension scheme, this is usually the best option. This is because most company pension schemes will involve the company making contributions as well as the workers, which means it makes your money go further and generates a bigger sum to invest. The employer might also pay for the administration of the scheme, which will reduce the money lost in charges.

In contrast, if you have a personal pension, it will be just your money going into the pot and any charges will be deducted from your payments. There are still tax benefits, as there are with all pensions, but there won't be the additional payments of an employer.

In broad terms, this means that if you want a pension and your employer is offering contributions, then this is going to be worth taking up. Of course we immediately slide into the treacle of ifs and buts, because different employers offer different schemes; however, in general terms employers' pension schemes are going to be worth considering before a personal pension.

As an example, the teachers' pension scheme takes 6 per cent of the salary of teachers, but it adds another 7.4 per cent, paid for by the employer. So that means that the amount of money being invested each month is more than doubled by the employer, which will mean much more being paid out than if pensioners were depending only on their own contributions. It's rowing with two oars rather than one.

A work-based pension should offer:

- a pension from the normal retirement age;
- annual increases to the pension once you retire;
- a tax-free lump sum at retirement;
- the possibility of retiring earlier on a reduced pension;
- a pension for early retirement due to ill health;
- pensions for your widow/er and other dependants if you die;
- life insurance which pays out a lump sum if you die.

Daft names, but it's still important

There are two main types of pension that you're likely to encounter in work-based schemes – or 'occupational' pensions as they are often called. (It's a term I've always associated with 'occupational therapy', which doesn't really inspire much optimism in a subject that's gloomy enough.) They are final salary and money purchase, neither of which labels gives much away.

The *final salary* scheme means that your pension will be based on a proportion of your salary at the time you retire (perhaps a sixtieth or an eightieth), multiplied by the number of years you've belonged to the pension scheme.

The advantage of this is that the company is promising that your pension will depend on your earnings and length of service, rather than on the vagaries of the stock market. So even if the investments haven't worked out, you'll still receive an assured amount.

With a *money purchase* scheme, there is no assured link between what you're earning when you retire and how much you'll receive in your pension. Instead, your contributions and the employer's contributions will be invested and whatever this amount has grown to when you retire is usually used to buy an annuity fund, which will pay out your pension. And there is also likely to be a lump sum payment, which you receive when you retire.

With the final salary scheme, the company is in effect promising to make up for any investment shortfalls, so that your pension isn't going to depend on market performance. But with a money purchase scheme the performance of your invested contributions will influence how much you end up receiving each month in your pension. Also determining the amount you receive will be the state of the annuities market. Once you've bought your annuity, this will shape how much you receive from this pension for the rest of your life.

Annuities

Annuities are a case of buying money with money. The amount you've accumulated in your pension over the years is used to buy an annuity, which in return for a lump sum will promise to deliver a payment every month until you die.

You don't have to buy an annuity from your pension company and, as with any financial product, it's worth shopping around for the best deals available. The range between the highest and lowest paying annuities can mean a difference of up to 20 per cent in terms of how much pensioners receive each month.

There are different types of annuity, with more features and benefits usually corresponding with lower monthly payments. There are *level annuities*, which means that the pension remains the same regardless of how long you live. To guard against inflation, there are *increasing annuities*, which increase payouts each year. *With-profits annuities* can increase over time, but that is dependent on investment performance.

Guaranteed annuity means that even if you die the day after you collect your first pension payment, your relatives can carry on receiving the pension for a set number of years afterwards. And a *joint annuity* means that if a husband or wife dies, the surviving person will continue to receive the pension for their rest of their lives.

The whole question of annuities seems set for scrutiny in the future. Low interest rates and longer life expectancy have contributed to a long-term decline in annuity rates, which has prompted questions about looking for other ways of funding retirement. In particular, there have been complaints that pensioners are pushed into putting all their pension money into annuities at a time when they don't appear to be offering great value, and that once an annuity is bought, there is no money left to be passed on to relatives. Pensioners can be upset that their pension pot might be worth hundreds of thousands of pounds, but their income from the annuity is a modest fraction of this.

Annuities have become the most widely used way of converting private money purchase schemes into monthly pensions, but up until the age of 75 you can defer buying an annuity and opt to draw your income directly from the pension fund (known as 'income drawdown'). Once pensioners are 75 years old, pension rules require that their pension pots are used to buy annuities, an obligation that rankles with some pension reformers.

This is an area to watch for changes and it's certainly worth taking specialist advice, looking at your particular circumstances and the amounts you have put into your pension, before making any decisions.

Topping-up

This is a way of fattening up your pension, by adding more than the regular monthly amount. These 'additional voluntary contributions' (AVCs) might be useful for people who started a pension late in their working lives or who are worried that their existing pension is going to leave them a little threadbare.

Group personal pensions

These are a mix of a personal and work-based pension. It usually means that a company has negotiated a group scheme for its employees and might make an employer's contribution – but the pensions themselves are personal pensions.

Personal pensions

These are pensions that operate separately from your work or any other state provision. Wherever you're working, you can take your personal pension with you – and this portability was one of the chief selling points when this new breed of pension first became available in the late 1980s.

The association between personal pensions and the high tide of yuppiedom hasn't been a happy one, with the image of the commission-crazed salesman still dogging personal pensions. But for people who are self-employed or don't have access to a workplace scheme, personal pensions provide an important alternative.

Personal pensions can provide the package of benefits usually associated with a work-based scheme, such as life insurance and provision for early retirement due to ill health. But whatever you get with a personal pension, you'll be paying for – choosing à la carte rather than getting the set menu.

Personal pensions are money purchase schemes and, as with work-based money purchase schemes, will be dependent on the fortunes of their investments. If they perform well, you'll get more in your pension. If they perform badly, you might have to revise your holiday plans.

Charges will also influence how much you get back of the money you've invested, so take a careful note of the charges in the schemes on offer. And remember that if you have to stop paying into a personal pension for a few months, the charges will continue to chew away at whatever you've invested. This is the kind of pension hell you want to avoid, where you've tipped a load of money into a pension and then, perhaps because you've lost your job or fallen ill, it's eaten by the piranhas of charges and administration costs.

With both the final salary and money purchase schemes, there is usually a tax-free lump sum paid when you retire, after which your pension becomes a regular payment, usually dependent on what your annuity can deliver.

Stakeholders

Stakeholder pensions were introduced in an attempt to make private pensions accessible to a wider range of people. This included those who wanted an affordable pension but didn't have access to the kind of group schemes available for people at work, or those working in places where there were no pension schemes.

Among the groups that stakeholder pensions were meant to reach out to were parents who had left work to raise children, people working on contracts, the self-employed, part-time workers and those on low to middle incomes who previously thought pensions were too expensive.

There are two key selling points for stakeholders: they have to be flexible and the charges have to be low. The flexibility means that you can start and stop payment, which is vital if you're not in regular full-time employment. If you're working on a series of temporary contracts, you might only want to contribute money when you're earning. And if a company wants to sell a stakeholder pension, it has to promise to keep the charges low, up to a limit of 1 per cent per year, which means that money invested isn't all going to disappear into commissions to keep the sales rep in flashy cufflinks.

It is still difficult to judge whether stakeholders, launched in April 2001, will be a long-term success. There remains a suspicion about private pensions, which will take a great deal of shifting, and there were initial signs that some of the most enthusiastic users of stakeholder pensions were wealthy grandparents buying them as investments for their grandchildren. But if you are looking for a pension which should be good value and which can be started with very small regular savings, perhaps only £20 a month, then ask about a stakeholder.

As well as individual stakeholder pensions, all but the smallest companies now have to offer group schemes under the stakeholder banner. Employers won't necessarily contribute to these pensions, but they will be able to arrange deductions from pay packets and there should be better value in schemes for a larger number of people.

However, while the stakeholder pension offers more people the chance to have a pension, it isn't a magic wand. Even though the concept has been introduced by the government, it's a private pension offered by commercial investment companies – and whatever you get out of it will reflect the amount you put in.

Here are some questions suggested by the Financial Services Authority to ask someone selling you a pension:

- Must I pay regularly or can I vary my contributions?
- What happens if I can't keep up my contributions?
- How much of my investments will be taken by charges?
- How much commission will you get from selling me this plan?
- Are you prepared to give up part of your commission to me (called a commission rebate)?
- What sort of investments would be most suitable for me, given the length of time until I retire, the way I feel about risk, and so on?
- At what age can I start to take my pension? Can I change this age without penalty?
- What are the penalties if later on I want to switch my plan to another provider or to a stakeholder pension scheme?

And I would suggest that when the personal pensions salesman sits down to explain pension plans, remember:

- He is trying to sell you something.
- This doesn't just *seem* complicated, it *is* complicated.

- There's no reason why you should understand it, so ask lots of questions.
- Slip into your questions buzzwords such as 'mis-selling scandal', 'the Maxwell pensioners' and 'Equitable Life'.
- He won't be around when you collect your pension, so make sure you know what you're being offered.
- He might not even be alive when you collect your pension, so he won't be around to take any complaints.
- Ask him what happens if you drop dead the day before you retire? Or the day after?
- And what happens if you get injured or too sick to work before you retire?
- What happens if the insurance company goes bust or is taken over?
- Ask him why he shows you his laptop computer as if you've never seen one before.

Pensions by other means

If you want cash to keep you when you stop working, then it needn't necessarily be a traditional pension.

For instance, instead of putting the money into a pension plan, there are people who have bought second houses, with the money that would have gone into a pension fund paying off a mortgage. By the time they reach retirement age, the mortgage will be cleared and the property can be sold, generating either a lump sum for a spending spree or money for further investment.

But again this depends on having the kind of spare cash necessary for such speculation. Also, unless your crystal ball is in full working order, it's impossible to know what kind of shape the housing market might be in when you want to retire.

Ten things about pensions to dazzle your friends

- There are 11 million state pensioners – 7 million women, 4 million men.

- The average state pension entitlement for men is £89.81 per week.

- A fifth of the population is of pensionable age.

- A second state pension scheme is scheduled for 2002.

- The state earnings related pension scheme (SERPS) is to be phased out.

- In 1909 the old age pension was five shillings a week.

- Personal pensions were launched in 1988.

- Annuities rates have halved in a decade.

- There are calls to scrap compulsory take-up of annuities at 75.

- Stakeholder schemes are compulsory for most employers.

- Ethical pensions are available which do not invest in environmentally-unfriendly companies.

Fear and loathing in my bank account

Modern money: I know I'm probably heading for the workhouse, but...

Maria, aged 36, is a freelance sub-editor, married with two children at primary school.

There always seems to be something that I have to buy this month. The car insurance is up for renewal, or the central heating needs fixing, or the credit card needs clearing. So the month when I can begin to think of starting a pension always seems to slip away.

My husband works full time and he has a pension from work. But I do worry that if anything happened, say if we split up, then I could be in a precarious position. And I know I should have organized a pension a long time ago, when it would have been cheaper. But since I don't have a work pension I can join, now I'm looking at stakeholder pensions.

Apart from the expense of private pensions, I've just not been completely sure about them, and you always fear that there might be a problem, and all that money that you could do with right now could be wasted. I'm probably just making excuses for putting it off so long, but I have been balancing this suspicion of pensions and the growing likelihood that I might spend my old age in the workhouse.

There's also something about the thought of pensions that makes me want to avoid the subject. It's the financial equivalent of the dentist's chair. You don't want to go, but you know in the long run it will be worse if you don't.

And there's something about looking so far ahead that can make it seem unreal. I don't feel like a pensioner, I'm not sure I want to be a pensioner. But at the same time, the years get faster and faster, and 20 years will pass so quickly – and then I'll be depending on whatever decisions I take now.

But it is so difficult. When you're knackered and the kids are rampaging, and you get out a holiday brochure, you start feeling as though you need a break more than anything else in the world. Or the car breaks down again and you need to borrow to replace it. And then I also want to start a pension – and you have to weigh up which is the bigger emergency. I'll have to decide soon before it's too late.

6

Borrowing – neither a borrower nor a lender be. Yeah, right

My bank account has developed a kind of tidal system, with the high tide beginning at payday, followed by a gradual emptying through the month, until the cycle begins again.

Every month I draw up plans to try to stop this leaking-bucket effect, even going as far on occasions as to consider Saving Money. I know this might sound far-fetched, but there are people who manage to end a month with more than they began. I've struggled to save money myself, but at least drawing up plans and making lists keeps me feeling optimistic that it might happen. It might not change anything, but it's a useful kind of displacement activity.

> Borrowing makes the world go round. Without it we wouldn't be able to afford houses, cars, Christmas or even that self-destructive spending spree in the days before your pay cheque hits your bank account.

What has all this got to do with borrowing?

The speed at which my bank account empties each month isn't really about spending. If it were just spending money I'd have nothing to complain about. The idea of spending

Fear and loathing in my bank account

my own money on myself now seems a distant prospect, like being a teenager again when my only outlays were on records (then known to young hipsters as LPs), alcohol and unfortunate choices of clothing.

No, what turns my bank account into a financial colander is my borrowing. As quickly as I shovel money into the account, it's emptied by a mortgage, personal loan, car loan and a credit card. And no matter how much I've shovelled into the account throughout my working life, there always seems to be the same set-up, just bigger money going in and bigger money going out and nothing left for me. Of course at some point in history I must have paid off a personal loan. But about a nanosecond afterwards I'd start borrowing all over again – and usually borrowing even larger sums than before.

How does this loop tape happen? It can be explained by *The Big Bill and No Savings Theory.* Sorry to get technical, but it happens like this. You've just paid off the loan that you'd taken out some time in the mid-19th century. And almost immediately your car breaks down and the garage tells you that it's terminal. You need a new car. Your family are baying to be driven places. You don't have any savings because you've been paying off all those loans – and everywhere you look there are adverts for loans. I once counted 40 separate offers of loans either in advertising or sent in the post to me in a single week.

So after a token phase of trying to see if there is any way around this impasse, you realize that you're going to have to borrow again. And the amount you plan to borrow has its own strange way of expanding the nearer you get to the point of agreeing a loan. Nothing outrageous, but because it's not quite real money you'll hike up your spending by another grand. Because you need that car or that holiday or that new furniture. In any other context £1,000 would be a vast sum, but when it's being borrowed and it's expressed as a modest increase in a monthly repayment over five years, it suddenly feels like small change. The end result is that you get back on the *borrowing treadmill,* with more of your salary disappearing each month into debts.

Of course when we're being bombarded with loan adverts we never hear about debts. There is no such word as 'debt' in this world of happy lending. What banks say they're offering is freedom and flexibility. You can have what you want, all you have to do is ask. In this high gloss vision of the world, families leap around on beaches or smile at each other in silent ecstasy, celebrating the fact that they've borrowed a great wedge of money – with no chance of paying it back for years.

If we were to see something closer to the truth, it would be a whole load of depressed-looking people around messy kitchen tables, realizing that they were never going to save anything and whose overdrafts had swollen to the size of Canada – but who still needed to borrow more.

Borrowing makes the world go round. Without it we wouldn't be able to afford houses, cars, Christmas or even that self-destructive spending spree in the days before your pay cheque hits your bank account.

When we talk about a standard of living, we're often really talking about a standard of borrowing, because in our credit culture it's our ability to borrow – our level of credit worthiness – that determines how much we can spend. Almost no one has enough cash in hand to buy a house or a new car, all we have is the capacity to borrow. And for people with the least amount of money, being unable to borrow from conventional lenders becomes one of the biggest practical problems in their financial lives.

When you talk about personal finance, people often start quoting 'rules' about borrowing – never borrow to pay off debt and never use a credit card to pay off another credit card and that kind of wise old owl stuff. This is all very well, in a pub know-all kind of way, but the real rules are much crueller and simpler. The first rule is that the more you have, the easier and cheaper it is to borrow. And the less you have, the more difficult and expensive it becomes to borrow. The second rule is that whatever deal you're offered, borrowing is always going to cost money – it's just a question of limiting how much.

Whatever your circumstances, you don't want to pay more for your borrowing than is necessary. So don't follow my own terrible example – and instead find a way of taking control of your borrowing.

Know the enemy: what to look out for in a loan

First, you want to pay as little in interest and charges as possible. So think of a loan as something you are buying, something with a definite cost. Don't think of what you're going to spend the money on, think of the money in cold hard terms. When you're taking out a loan, you're buying money – and you want as low a price tag as possible.

The factors that you'll need to compare will be:

- interest rates;
- length of repayment period;
- total cost of repayments;
- charges;
- insurance;
- whether the loan is secured against your home;
- any penalties if you want to pay off the loan ahead of schedule.

The interest is going to be the main cost of the loan, and no matter what type of loan you're taking out it's worth shopping around, because there are large variations in rates.

If you've found what you hope will be a good deal, you need to start considering the length of time over which you want to pay back the loan. *Paying off the loan as soon as possible is going to reduce the amount of interest you pay.* But the monthly repayments have to be affordable.

This has got be a real-world calculation, rather than the 'Next week I'll be famous so it doesn't matter' type of financial planning. If the arrangement is over several years, you have to be sure that there are no financial icebergs on the horizon – such as the risk of being made redundant or your plans to scrap the day job and become a pavement artist. If you want to examine how much monthly repayments can be affected by the length of the loan, there are Internet sites with 'loan calculators' that will let you see the differences (see Chapter 10 for some suggested sites).

If you get into trouble with repayments it's a long and depressing road back to recovery. If you default on a loan for goods such as a car, you'll end up by losing the car and still owing money. Or if it's cash you've borrowed and you start to struggle with repayments, you could end up paying more and more in interest without ever clearing what you've borrowed. If a personal loan is secured against something you don't want to lose, such as your house, you could be heading for even deeper water, so make sure you know what you could lose if you default.

On a more upbeat note, you could save yourself a few quid if you were able to pay off a loan early. There are 'flexible' loans, which are no more expensive than other loans, but which allow you to over-pay without incurring any penalties. This can leave your options open and, a couple of years into a loan, if your finances improve, you'll be able to pay off the balance and reduce the overall amount of interest.

How do different types of borrowing compare?

There are more exceptions than rules to what's the cheapest form of borrowing. In the past, credit cards were seen as an expensive way to borrow, but competition between lenders saw credit cards becoming one of the cheapest types of credit. And then prices started to go up again – and it might be that a personal loan is a better deal. Within each type of borrowing – credit card, overdraft or personal loan – there are wide variations too, so you'll have to look closely at what is the best deal at the time.

For example, here's a snapshot of borrowing deals available in October 2001:

- Credit card – Co-operative: 9.8 per cent; Barclaycard: 19.4 per cent.
- Fixed rate mortgage – Britannia: 4.44 per cent.
- Overdraft – Barclays: 15.6 per cent; Nationwide FlexAccount: 9.9 per cent.
- Personal loan – Co-operative: 8.4 per cent; Tesco: 9.1 per cent.
- Store cards – Mothercare: 29 per cent; John Lewis: 13 per cent.

How do these loans work?

Personal loans

If you're looking to borrow a larger amount of cash, probably thousands rather than hundreds of pounds, then the most likely loan will be a 'personal loan' or 'bank loan'. Unlike a credit card, these loans have fixed repayments over a set number of months or years – so you know exactly when the debt will be cleared, how much you'll pay each month and how much you will have paid in interest.

In terms of comparing interest with other types of borrowing, personal loans tend to be more expensive than a mortgage, but cheaper than a credit card or an overdraft, although the introductory rates of credit cards can be lower.

These loans are typically for particular spending plans, such as buying a car, getting married, installing over-priced kitchens, turning your back bedroom into a cyber-office or any other project that needs money up front that you don't have. While credit cards tend to soak up the flexible borrowing for unexpected events (like Christmas), the personal loans are more likely to be used for planned spending.

Arranging such a loan no longer involves having to fawn all over the bank manager – and you don't have to pretend that it's for something worthy like home improvements. You can arrange loans over the phone with a minimum of fuss and with very few questions asked as to what you want to do with the money. And if the lender approves your application, you can usually receive the cash within a few days.

Your own bank might offer you a preferential rate, but it's quite likely that another lender might be able to better what you've been offered. There are plenty of deals available so, as ever, if you shop around you'll find savings. When you're borrowing, there's no such thing as loyalty – go wherever you get the best offer.

Apart from the interest rate, the other consideration is the period of time for repayment. This can be anything between six months and 10 years – but the sooner you pay back the debt, the less interest you'll be paying. This is a question of finding the right balance, because even though it's a good idea to get rid of a debt as soon as possible, you don't want to place unrealistic pressures on your monthly income.

When you get quotes for repayments you'll probably have two tables showing monthly payments with and without insurance. There is no obligation to take out this insurance, which is intended to protect payments in the event of illness or redundancy, and you should make sure that you don't get bullied into signing up for something you don't really want.

If it's a longer term or larger loan, you might want to consider insurance. But you'll need to make sure that it's not too expensive: avoid finding a cheap interest rate only to lose the advantage by shelling out for over-priced insurance cover. Also, make sure you know what is included in the insurance: you don't want to find yourself thwarted by small print when you come to make a claim.

If it's a small or short-term loan you might want to consider whether you really need insurance. If you think you're about to lose your job, you probably shouldn't be borrowing anyway. And it's quite likely that there might be a clause in the insurance policy that means that if you lose your job you won't get a payout for the first 60 days. If you were making repayments over a year, this would mean that you were only usefully covered for 10 months.

Look to see what happens if you want to pay back a loan early. 'Flexible' loans should allow you to pay more than the agreed amount without any penalties, so that you can reduce the scheduled length of repayments or lower the amount paid each month. This can mean a decent saving on interest.

Overdrafts

Overdrafts are like old friends to me: they've seen me through bad times and, well, even worse times. We've been on holiday together, moved house, kept an elderly car on the road together, even married – and for years I never really asked how much they cost. Maybe that's because I didn't really think of it as borrowing, rather as a reserve for when the tank runs empty. I used my overdraft so often that I almost thought of it as part of the month's salary.

This was a bad idea – an overdraft is borrowing and that means it's going to cost money. And it can often mean paying a higher rate of interest than your credit card, and certainly will be higher than a personal loan. So if you hear people saying that they'd rather pay by cash, using their overdraft, rather than sticking a bill on the plastic, they could be paying out more and not less in interest.

As well as interest there can be other costs attached to going into the overdraft zone, such as having to pay bank charges. Many accounts don't make you pay charges as long as you stay in credit. But once you step over that invisible line, you can be paying for every cheque and withdrawal. And if you stray into an *unauthorized* overdraft, it's the banking equivalent of giving the biggest bouncer at a nightclub a playful slap. The rates of most banks for unauthorized overdrafts are punitively fixed at around 30 per cent APR – more even than the cash-shredding rates of some store cards. So if it looks as though you're not going to be able to live within the overdraft limit, then it's worth telling your bank in advance and asking for an extension, before they put more of your money in the blender.

If you're a student you should be able to get an account with an interest-free overdraft, so it's worth taking advantage of what is in effect an interest-free loan, rather than running up bills on a credit card.

The good overdraft guide:

- look for low interest;
- student accounts should have interest-free overdrafts;
- ask yourself whether a personal loan would be cheaper;
- avoid unauthorized overdrafts.

Credit cards

The growth in the credit card market, including new players arriving from the USA, has introduced plenty of competition. This has been good news for the consumer – and if you're canny and willing to play the field and able to keep control of spending, credit cards can be a decent form of borrowing.

If you get a card with a long interest-free period, and you have the self-discipline to keep clearing the card within this time limit, then you needn't pay anything for the temporary use of their cash. But of course credit cards make a fortune from people who always mean to pay off the cards but never quite manage it.

The next cheapest way of using a credit card is to take advantage of the introductory rates on offer from credit card companies. These so-called 'teaser' rates are designed to draw customers away from other cards and from other forms of borrowings – with the offer of bargain basement interest rates for three or six months or a year. But at the end of the introductory period, the interest rate will take a sharp upward hike. And, as another warning, many of these introductory offers only apply to balances transferred from elsewhere, and any new purchases with the cards are charged at the full standard rate.

As with any introductory offer, the intention is to attract customers with the hope that they'll stay beyond the end of the cheap deal and then be too lazy to move again. But, if you have the energy to be promiscuous with your credit cards, you can keep switching from card to card and keep paying very low rates of interest.

Whichever card you choose, their great virtue of flexibility is their greatest vice when you're paying them back. It's fine if you're paying for a shopping spree of a few hundred pounds, but if you run up a big bill on credit cards you have to be extremely disciplined with the repayments. In my own experience, I know it's so easy not to pay off the whole amount and gradually to allow the balance to drift upwards, and then to find yourself shelling out interest payments each month.

The headline interest rate might have drawn you in, but if you don't pay back what you've borrowed for years and years, you could end up paying much more.

Mortgages

The idea of getting involved with mortgages when you're not even moving house might seem like punishing yourself unnecessarily. But that's probably because the memory of the angst of finding a mortgage was wrapped up with the pressures of house hunting and the feeling that everyone was helping themselves to your money. But extending your current mortgage, or getting a bigger mortgage with another lender, is much less difficult when you're not moving house. And it can be the most affordable way of borrowing large sums – maybe £10,000 and upwards.

Mortgage repayments are stretched out over anything from 10 to 25 years which, with comparatively low interest rates, makes for low monthly repayments. Of course, the downside is that your total repayment over the years will be a larger amount. There is also the important point to remember that, unlike personal loans, if you over-stretch yourself and default on repayments you're at risk of losing your home.

Such health warnings apart, the rise in property prices has meant that many people have houses that are now much more valuable than the size of their original mortgage. Tapping into this 'equity' tied up in your house might be the most cost-effective way of borrowing.

If you're looking for £20,000 or so in a personal loan, you could be facing some hefty repayments, but if you add it to your mortgage it's a much lower monthly charge. But nothing is for nothing, and this would still mean that you lose £20,000 from your profit when you come to sell.

The process of getting a larger mortgage is simple enough – especially if you're staying with your current lender. They already have many details about you from your previous application and it's a much more straightforward business than getting a mortgage from scratch. Again, most of the work of applying can be carried out with a few phone calls (and then it's only a small matter of 25 years of repayments).

Credit unions

I've had my fair share of irritating letters from bank managers, but so far none of them has written threatening to smash down my door and take my television away if I didn't pay them back. Such robust approaches to debt recovery – favoured by your local loan sharks – are what can happen if people can't get credit from a bank or building society, but still need cash in a hurry.

If you're unemployed, elderly or if you live in one of the 1.5 million households that don't have a bank account (that's an estimated 3.5 million adults) it can be difficult to borrow from conventional sources. In this gap the credit union movement is beginning to make a substantial impression, with about 300,000 members. Credit unions are non-profit making community banking organizations, financial cooperatives, which provide low-cost borrowing and saving services. Members make regular savings each month and in return gain access to affordable and flexible credit, aimed particularly at helping tide people over short-term requirements for relatively small sums of money.

Credit unions have in the past been based around something that members have in common, such as working for the same company or in the same industry. But now the regulations have been widened and they can be open to something as broadly defined as living or working in the same city. For example, there is now a credit union serving the population of Leeds.

Before being able to borrow, members of the credit union have to save for at least three months, and then borrowing is limited to two and a half times savings. Repayments for credit unions are made at a rate of 12.65 per cent APR and savings yield a maximum 8 per cent annual dividend.

Credit unions have been seen as an important step towards financial self-reliance for individuals and communities, and they have often been associated with community action groups. For example, the Derry Credit Union in Northern Ireland was co-founded by 23-year-old John Hume in 1960, before he became involved in politics. From a kitty of £7 it has grown to hold savings worth £42 million. 'It provides ordinary working people and the unemployed with the chance to make the maximum use of their money. It's a strictly cooperative movement, totally non-profit making and run by ordinary people themselves,' he says of the Derry Credit Union, which he has described as the 'most successful cooperative in Ireland'.

But credit unions are ambitious to develop into a practical and competitive alternative to conventional banking. With plans for more credit unions to set up high street offices, they would like to take the place in the community of the disappearing bank and building society branches.

Car loans

When I think about car loans, I always think about the smell of new cars. You know that smell you get when you're at the garage, waiting to collect your own dusty vehicle after a service, and you begin looking lustfully at the smart new models in the showroom. Almost surreptitiously, you ease open the door of a car you can't afford, and you're hit by that smell of upholstery and factory-fresh paint and plastics. You look at a row of controls across the dashboard and that unturned wheel, and think how good it would be to have a car in which everything worked. That's how I think of car loans, which is a terrible place to start, because I should really just be thinking about the loan as a lump of cash that I'm paying interest to borrow.

If you want to buy a car, new or second-hand, there are two main routes. You can borrow the money from a bank or credit company, or else you can use the finance deals offered by the car manufacturer or dealer.

If you're borrowing from the bank, there might be something called a 'car loan', but that's usually just packaging for what is a straightforward personal loan. Whether you call it a car loan, wedding loan or home improvement loan, it still means a schedule of repayments over an agreed number of years, like any other loan. There are advantages with a personal loan – you know how much you've borrowed and when the debt will be cleared. And because there are plenty of lenders competing for business, you should get a good deal.

If you buy a car from the manufacturer you have more options, but not necessarily better value, even though there might be imaginative claims about what great deals are on offer. Taking a snapshot in the autumn of 2001, while car manufacturers' deals are charging in the region of 14 per cent interest, there are personal loans available for less than 10 per cent.

In newspapers you'll often see adverts saying you can drive away a new car for £99 a month or whatever. But these deals are almost always more complicated, with the headline figure usually representing only part of the purchase price. Before you can get your £99 a month deal, you might have to put down a deposit of £5,000. Which isn't quite how the advert seemed at first glance.

Car finance also often makes claims about interest-free credit. Call me old fashioned if you like, but I tend to think of interest-free credit as meaning that you don't pay any interest on the purchase. But in car finance, this usually means that you don't pay any interest if you put down a 30 or 40 per cent deposit. Which really means that you're getting interest-free credit only on part of the car.

As car sellers look for the lowest headline monthly payment figures, they can end up with some very convoluted systems of charges. To achieve the £99 a month for a new car, with interest-free credit, might involve an initial deposit, a period of repayments and then a final payment at the end. And, of course, you're not really paying any less, because car manufacturers' interest rates are often higher than the best personal loans.

In another attempt to keep down the monthly payments for a new or nearly-new car, dealers are offering 'personal contract purchases' (or PCPs), in which buyers put down a deposit on the car and then make a series of monthly repayments over an agreed period of time. The amount to be paid is calculated on how much the car is projected to be worth at the end of the agreement. At the end of the arrangement, you can either pay to buy the car outright or give the car back. In this sense, the arrangement could almost be seen as a hybrid of buying and leasing. The advantage of this system is that you can get behind the wheel of a new car for lower monthly payments, but if you want to fully own the car, then it's not cheaper in the long run.

Another option for buying a car is hire purchase, in which a set number of payments are made until the price of the car, plus interest, is fully paid. Unlike a personal loan, ownership of the car does not pass to the buyer until all the debt has been cleared.

Credit checking

Whenever we apply for any kind of loan we're told there will be a credit check. But what does it mean? Do you get a mark out of 10? Is there a black-edged list of dodgy debtors? Is there a team of investigators who ring round banks and previous lenders to see if you're to be trusted?

The main assessment used is 'credit scoring'. Each lender will have its own formula, but the basic principle is to award points according to the results of a series of questions that examine your ability to make repayments and any evidence of problems in the past.

These look at how much you earn, where you live, how long you've been in your job, how long you've been at your current address, whether you're a homeowner and how much you're already paying out on other debts. And if your score shows you to be a low credit risk, you cross the winning line and can borrow money.

It's like calculating the odds on a horse race, with the lenders trying to work out whether it's worth the risk of giving someone credit. Even if you have a steady income, this might be outweighed by negatives, such as not being on the electoral roll because you've just moved, or if you're already overloaded with debts.

A key piece of information that is likely to be checked by every credit card company considering an application is the 'credit reference'. Anyone who has ever had a loan, mortgage, store card or credit card will have a credit reference file, which holds details of all your borrowing. When people warn you against getting a bad credit history, this is where the lenders find out where the bodies are buried. As well as holding your credit history, the credit file will have details of anyone with the same surname living at the same address. So if a relative living with you has debt problems, the lenders will have that information as well.

Credit card companies don't hold their own credit references, instead they use independent agencies. The biggest of these agencies are Experian and Equifax, which hold files on about 44 million people at about 25 million addresses.

Ten things about borrowing to dazzle your friends

- There is £700 billion outstanding in credit and borrowing.

- Nine out of ten consumers say borrowing is too easy.

- Six out of ten adults are repaying borrowed money.

- In a single month, £14.9 billion in mortgages is approved.

- Mark Twain, Jan Vermeer and Ulysses S Grant were all bankrupts.

- Donation cards usually pass on 0.25 per cent of purchases.

- There are 22 million store cards in circulation, often with interest rates twice as high as credit cards.

- If you want to withdraw money without your partner knowing, supermarket cashbacks can cover your tracks.

- Credit union members can borrow at 12.65 per cent.

- Student accounts usually offer interest-free overdrafts.

Under data protection legislation, anyone can see their own file (if you send a cheque for £2). If anything in these files is wrong, you can appeal to have an entry changed. And if this remains in dispute, you can add a 200-word note putting your side of the case or explaining any special circumstances, such as payments being missed because of illness or bereavement.

Modern money: why do you need money?

While we borrow more, worry more and get stressed out about our finances, there are others who have rejected money and choose instead to live without any possessions of their own.

'I can't own anything in my own name, I've no bank account in my own name,' says Sister Angela, a nun who lives in a community of five nuns in a Dublin housing estate.

Since joining the religious life in 1962, Sister Angela has maintained a vow of poverty, which has prevented her from having any possessions or money of her own. Everything that she has, down to the shoes she's wearing, belongs to the community. If she wants anything, she has to ask the other members of her order.

While the past 40 years have seen a revolution in the borrowing and spending power of many people, sisters in religious orders have remained outside the whole consumer culture. Sister Angela and her fellow nuns have a direct debit card, because it's safer than carrying cash, but as individuals they have never had credit cards, personal loans or any other kind of borrowing. All their dealings with money have been on a strictly utilitarian basis, providing for basic needs and the bills of the community, and with no scope for the sisters buying things for themselves. There is no personal finance. This has been a 'liberation', she says, allowing her to focus on her spiritual progress instead of her financial progress. 'Money isn't a priority.'

The community of nuns each year draws up a budget and each member submits a claim for her needs, in terms of her professional work and her own personal needs, such as clothes. If there is any extra money left over after the budgeting process, this is given away. It's a frugal life, but it's their choice and keeping out of the way of money allows them a freedom to pursue their religious life, Sister Angela says.

There are negatives to this communal life, she says. 'You can never choose the car you'd prefer, you never really have the furniture that you might want, you can't choose the holiday that you want.'

But arriving in the convent where she joined 40 years ago 'felt like coming home', and she says that choosing poverty, which most people would fear, has been a 'great gift'.

7
Insurance – the seven ages of man

In the same way that you can tell the age of trees by the number of rings in their trunk, you can probably guess the age of people by the number of insurance policies they've acquired.

When you're young and expecting to live forever, insurance is a remote world for sad grey old-timers. Then you get a car – and for the first time, you need insurance, which seems a huge imposition. Then when you're planning a trip somewhere faraway and

> *No one is going to stop you buying insurance that won't work when you try to use it. It's like buying a suit that's three sizes too small. You can buy it, but you're never going to be able to wear it.*

exotic, where fatal diseases are queuing up at the arrivals lounge to meet you, someone suggests travel insurance – and it seems like a good idea, so you get into the habit of insuring yourself for holidays. As the great wheel of time grinds on, you'll move into your own place – and with a mortgage, you'll need to get insurance for your possessions and for the building itself. And you'll probably end up with mortgage cover or life insurance, particularly if you've acquired a family. Then you start to notice in your bank statements that every other direct debit is for some type of insurance, whether it's payment protection on a loan or health cover to look after the secret hypochondriac that hides away within all of us.

Insurance is offered to us more than ever before. When you book a flight with a cut-price airline, you're always asked whether you want travel insurance. If you buy furniture with a credit deal, you'll be offered insurance on the loan as well as the stuff you're buying. Buy a washing machine – do you want insurance with that, sir? I'm waiting for the day that I buy a pizza and they ask me whether I want insurance as a side order.

This enthusiasm for insurance is because it can make money. For a discount airline selling seats for next to nothing, the insurance might be more profitable than the fare. The same can be the case with payment protection plans, which hike up the monthly payments and are often expensive for what they really cover.

When you're looking for insurance, the phrase you'll keep encountering is *peace of mind*, which is a feelgood way of presenting the concept of covering risk. But a more appropriate way of looking at insurance is to think of it as *gambling*, with the insurance company operating as the bookie. When you go on holiday without insurance, you're gambling that you won't need medical care or you won't have anything stolen or broken. If you get home unscathed, you'll have saved yourself the insurance.

If you do take out cover, the insurance company is working out the odds on you needing to claim – and the price of the insurance premium is calculated accordingly, the same way that a bookie might work out the odds on a horse winning a race. And just as a bookie prices in the factors that might be relevant, such as previous form, the conditions and the other horses running, so the insurer builds a picture based on all its previous experience of the likelihood of a punter needing to claim. And each individual insurance policy is part of a bigger picture of millions of other gambles being taken by travellers, drivers, homeowners and whoever else is being insured.

As well as the insurance company making its own calculations about our chances of crashing a car or being burgled, the other side of the equation is our own attitude to risk. There are people who feel better if they go through life padded up with insurance and ready to fend off whatever bouncers life bowls at them. Other people see insurance as a sign of personal weakness and like to sail close to the wind. In either case, a difficulty is often that insurance is seen as a general protection, an emotional state of mind rather than a very specific contract. When people say, 'I've got insurance', it's a bit like saying, 'I've got money' – which means nothing until you know how much.

Whether you're insured in every direction, or have less cover than a string bikini, you should know in advance what you're going to be able to recover if you need to claim. One of the biggest complaints about insurance is that people think they are covered for items that aren't included.

If you're booking a cheap flight and you agree to insurance, what does that mean? The person selling it probably doesn't really know and if they do they don't have time to tell you. So you head off into the sun feeling insured – and then when you get into difficulty you might find that the policy has very specific limits on cover. For instance, you might have a medical condition that will worsen when you're away and you might need hospital treatment, which is going to be very expensive. And when you get home and try to claim, you'll find that pre-existing medical conditions are excluded from the cover and you'll get nothing.

The difficulty is that *no one is going to stop you buying insurance that won't work when you try to use it*. It's like buying a suit that's three sizes too small. You can buy it, but you're never going to be able to wear it. This might sound rather perverse, but the test for a policy's appropriateness often only really arises when you try to claim.

The way to avoid problems, apart from reading the small print, is to keep asking questions. And if you can find an insurer you trust, then ask what will be most appropriate for your specific needs, which means disclosing all relevant information, such as your health or any other factors that could affect risk.

There are insurance brokers who might also be able to find an insurer that specializes in the specifics of your particular need. For instance if you have a medical condition that makes life insurance difficult or expensive, they might know of a company that has handled such cases. And there is never any harm in asking.

Motor insurance: mirror, signal, oh bugger

Insuring your car has become steadily more expensive in the last few years, with the price driven upwards by an increase in claims, which has been attributed in part to the 'compensation culture'. This means that every victim of a minor collision expects to be treated for emotional distress by a team of psychologists in a private Swiss clinic.

Whatever the reason, we're all paying considerably more to keep our wheels on the road. And we would all like to find ways to pay less – which means identifying the factors that determine the premium. These are going to include:

- where you live;
- where the car is parked;
- your age, gender and occupation;
- who else will be driving the car;
- your past claims record;
- if you have any drink driving convictions;
- the engine size, make and value of the car;
- security on the car;
- annual mileage;
- whether the car will be used for work.

These are not always items you can change, but you can try to turn them to your advantage. For instance, there could be a *specialist provider* for your occupation or something else that makes you distinct from the common driving herd. For instance, if you're a teacher, Eagle Star offers a discount. If you're a pensioner, Saga might be able to offer a customized deal.

The *no-claims bonus* discount can also vary. At the moment, the Halifax's insurance arm, esure, has been offering a higher rate of discount to drivers with 10 years without any claims. This reflects the fact that insurance companies are looking to narrow down markets to lower-risk drivers. Women are better risks than men, older drivers are better risks than young. It's not that women have fewer accidents, but they have less serious accidents, which in insurance terms means they are less expensive for insurance companies.

Whatever the cost, motor insurance isn't optional: it's required by the Road Traffic Act and not to have insurance is an offence.

The main types of insurance that you'll come across will be *third party*, which covers injuries to other people and damage to their property, or *third party, fire and theft*, which will be more expensive and is likely to include an excess, but means that in addition to third party cover you will have cover for the car being stolen.

These types of policies will cover your legal obligation to have insurance, but it means that your own car isn't covered. This might make sense if you have an old banger that is worth less than the cost of insuring it. But it means that if you have an accident and can't claim against the other driver, then you have to cover your own expenses.

The most widely used form of insurance is *comprehensive*, which will cover you and your own car as well as anyone else involved in an accident. Other benefits could include a personal accident benefit, medical expenses and cover for any personal effects damaged in an accident. This type of insurance is more expensive than third party.

Here are Diamond Insurance's tips for cutting the cost of car insurance:

- Voluntary excess: taking a higher excess than the standard £100 could give motorists a substantial discount on their premium.
- Many people already avoid making claims for lower cost accidents to protect their no-claims bonus, which can be worth hundreds of pounds. So, on balance, it might be worth considering taking a higher excess.
- Take more tests: if you have passed your test in the last year, you can take a follow-on test called Pass Plus. Some insurers will give you a discount for this.
- More experienced drivers can also reduce their premiums by passing the Institute of Advanced Motorists advanced driving test.
- Low mileage and limited use: telling your insurer how many miles you do, especially if it's below average, can drive premiums down.

- Use off-street parking: using a garage or driveway at night rather than leaving your car on the street will attract a discount with most insurers.
- Security: insurers prefer prevention rather than claims, so vehicles fitted with an engine immobilizer or alarm may qualify for a discount.
- Drive a smaller car: as well as being cheaper to buy and more economical to run, smaller cars cost less to insure.
- Use the Internet: many insurers offer a 5 to 10 per cent discount on policies purchased over the Internet.
- Shop around: this is probably the most vital means of keeping your premiums down. Increasing specialization in the insurance industry means it's more important than ever to make your calls to the type of insurer who will be able to offer you the best deal for your particular circumstances.

Contents insurance

The Association of British Insurers defines 'contents' as anything in the house that you'd take when you moved. So it's furniture, the television, jewellery, the fridge, your clothes... well, you get the picture. It's your possessions. And the cover will be against a series of calamities, such as fire, theft, floods, flooded washing machines, accidental breakages and storms.

But as has been said before, insurance isn't a general principle, it's a specific contract – and what is and isn't insured and how you will be compensated depends on what you've agreed. So before signing up to the cheapest contents insurance you're offered, find out what is included and excluded.

Among the areas to examine are *whether personal possessions are covered when you're away from home*. If you lose your fancy new laptop computer when you're on the train, is it covered by your contents insurance? There are policies that allow you to extend cover beyond the home.

And when you claim, are you going to be receiving the *replacement value* for items lost? Or will you be paid the value that the lost items would have made in their present state – which is going to be considerably less. It's worth investigating before you find out the hard way.

It's also important to find out whether there are any *maximum limits on individual items*. If you're keeping a collection of hugely expensive paintings in your back bedroom, the best time to tell the insurer isn't the day after they've been stolen. So ask in advance about whether you need any special valuations or security precautions for expensive items.

If you want to save money on your contents insurance, then take a look at what might make insurers think of you as being a safer bet. This might include *improving security*, such as adding burglar alarms or putting locks on windows. And you might get a discount if you get your buildings insurance from the same provider.

A large factor in how much you pay will be *where you live*. If you live in an inner city area, in a high-crime postcode, then you'll be paying more. And if you live in the highest-crime areas you might find insurers refusing to offer insurance at any price. Insurers base their premiums on the history of claims from an area and this means that in practice the poorest people, living in the poorest areas with the highest crime rates and in greatest need of insurance, will be paying the most for their insurance.

When quoting for cover, insurers look at the postcode in which you live and where it ranks in their bands of risk. There are about 25 different bands, covering the spectrum from dodgiest to safest addresses, and covering all 1.5 million postcodes. This ranking of risk will have a big influence on how much you're charged, with premiums for the 'worst' postcodes costing as much as six times the prices charged for insurance in the 'best' postcodes.

Buildings insurance

If contents insurance applies to things in a house that you'd take when you moved, buildings insurance is about covering the stuff that stays put, such as the walls, the bath and the doors. It's about the fabric of the building – and the basic calculation for the sum to be insured is based on *how much the property would cost to rebuild*. It isn't based on how much you could get for the property, but how much it would cost to physically re-build.

While contents insurance is optional, if you buy a house with a mortgage the lender will require you to take out buildings insurance – although you're under no obligation to buy their policy.

Buildings insurance will cover damage from domestic disasters such as fires and floods. But if you get to that other grim reaper of subsidence, the matter isn't so straightforward. This is a case of looking very carefully at the small print to see if a policy will cover subsidence-related claims. And if subsidence is included, look to see if there is an upper limit. If you can only claim £1,000 it isn't going to be anywhere near enough.

If you live in a flat, buildings insurance will probably need to be a collective policy for all the properties in the building. This is because if the walls start collapsing in your flat, it's not just going to be your problem. And you can't really calculate the re-building costs of a single flat in a block. So a management company, or whoever represents the leaseholders, will have to arrange a joint policy, which will cover shared areas such as the roof and the exterior.

Travel

Travel insurance seems to have become more widely available in recent years. Tour operators, airlines, travel Web sites, supermarkets and even insurance companies are all touting for your business. What they will all say is that they want to make sure that if your holiday ends in disaster – or for that matter doesn't begin because of disaster – at least you'll get your money back.

But make sure you know what you're getting, because travel insurance isn't about getting the cheapest, it's about getting what you need. If you buy a bargain insurance deal, maybe as part of a package holiday, it's going to be *no use to you if it doesn't provide cover where it's needed.* For instance, if you travel to the United States and end up needing hospital treatment, this is going to be very expensive – and it isn't the time to discover that it's not included in your policy.

You don't want to become a total insurance anorak, but it is worth looking at the small print to see what you're buying. Is there an upper limit on claiming for individual items? I knew someone who had a camcorder stolen on holiday and who couldn't believe that the travel insurance wouldn't pay up any more than £200 for a single item. But that was the contract that he'd signed.

The areas that are likely to be included and which should be checked out for usefulness are cover for:

- cancellation;
- delay;
- personal accident;
- medical expenses;
- personal belongings;
- legal expenses.

There will also be a list of *exclusions and exemptions* that are worth checking out. These can say that claims are invalidated if you were drunk or if you weren't paying adequate attention to your possessions. And you might find that any kind of dangerous sport is excluded from cover and will require additional insurance – and it's important to find out how 'dangerous sport' is defined.

As well as one-off insurance policies for a specific holiday, you can also buy *annual policies.* These can be better value if you take a few trips in a year – and they can be extended to take in other family members.

Private health insurance

Private health insurance has never really taken off in this country to the extent that might once have been expected. There are a large number of people who have a company health insurance scheme as a perk from their employer, but it still has a long way to go before it's a typical expenditure for individuals.

This might be a cultural aversion – and a certain loyalty to the National Health Service. But I suspect it's also because with private health insurance it's not always particularly clear what you're buying. And there's a strong suspicion among consumers that no matter what you're paying each month, if there's an emergency or you have a serious illness, you'll end up in the NHS anyway. It is the case that when you buy private health insurance, you're not buying into a parallel health system, with separate doctors and hospitals. Instead you're buying a complex set of benefits that work alongside the health service.

The biggest selling point is usually that you can avoid the long waiting lists for non-emergency treatment and operations. So instead of hanging around for months, you can fast-forward an appointment with a consultant and then can fix up a time for an operation.

As well as looking at what's included in your policy, take a look at the list of what is not covered. Here's an example taken from the health cover scheme of a big high street bank:

What is not covered

- Treatment for chronic or terminal conditions.
- All outpatients consultations after the initial consultation.
- Drugs, dressings and appliances not prescribed as part of your in-patient or day care treatment.
- Private GP visits, eye tests, dental treatment, vaccinations, screenings.
- Pregnancy and childbirth.
- Self-inflicted injuries.
- Injuries from professional sport.
- Drug or alcohol abuse.
- Cosmetic surgery.
- HIV and AIDS.

This is a pretty impressive opt-out clause. You begin to realize that the policy is addressing quite a narrow area of health and not the kind of all-embracing service that could be seen as an alternative to the NHS.

There are other areas in which health insurance is likely to not be able to help. If you have a pre-existing medical condition, such as diabetes, this might be excluded from cover. You can't blame insurers for this, because to make money they need to have some policyholders who will never need to claim. But it shows that health insurance shouldn't be confused with a health service.

Life insurance

There aren't many laughs in life insurance, the benefits of which are only reaped when someone dies. There's a certain grim humour in the way that people selling life insurance never actually like to use the word 'death'. There's a great deal of talk about 'passing away' and 'in the sad event that your loved one... er... should no longer... be alive'. The advertising is all very upbeat, focusing on how the people left behind will be looked after by the cash windfall that follows your death.

And that is the point of life insurance. If you pay the mortgage and bills or pay half the mortgage or whatever, your death would mean a sharp loss of income for your family – and life insurance would help to make up the shortfall. It's the kind of insurance that seems more important when you have dependants.

Life insurance has become a competitive market, which means that there is plenty of choice for consumers and shopping around is likely to be to your advantage. Unlike many financial products, it is not too difficult to make direct comparisons between the costs and benefits of life insurance, particularly so-called 'term insurance' (or 'term assurance', it's the same thing).

Term insurance is the cheapest and most commonly used form of life insurance – and the basic principle is that you pay a certain amount each month for a set number of years and if you die within that period your family will collect an agreed amount of money. If you're still alive at the end of the period, the policy ends and you don't get any money back. But at least you're still there. And if you stop paying the premiums, the policy stops and there are no refunds on what you've paid.

The amounts that your family will collect if you die often sound large, but think about how much they might really need: £100,000 would be a decent amount for a spending spree, but how does it compare with the loss of 10 years' earnings? Suddenly it doesn't seem as much, especially if you still owe money on a mortgage or loans.

How much you'll be asked to pay will depend on the perceived risks of you dying before the end of the insurance term. If the insurers think you're going to outlive the policy, it's going to be cheaper. So they will be looking at factors such as age, gender, health, whether you're a smoker and your occupation. If you're a middle-aged male chain-smoker with a bad heart who works as a stuntman, don't expect any bargains.

Term insurance has a number of variations (well, nothing's that simple with money). The most straightforward variety is called *level term*, which means that no matter at what point the insured person dies, they receive the same amount. So if you die the day before the policy ends or the day after it begins, you get the same money.

Another form of term insurance is *decreasing term*, which means that the amount paid out on death goes down each year of the policy. The idea behind this is that outgoings such as the mortgage will also be declining – and that the important time to have extra money would be if the insured person died in the early years of the policy. The policy can be set up to run parallel to a mortgage, so that it ends when the mortgage is paid off.

There is also *increasing term* insurance, which is designed to counter the gnawing away of inflation by providing a payment that will increase as the policy progresses.

Another way of keeping your options open is a *convertible term* policy, which means that you begin with term insurance but you can change later to other more comprehensive and more expensive forms of life insurance, such as whole-life insurance.

While term insurance has a set period for cover, maybe 20 years or whatever, *whole-life insurance* means that there will be a pay-out whenever you die – you're covered for the whole of your life. This is more expensive, because at some point the insurance company is going to have to pay out, and the only variation is when it happens. But it means that there will be a guaranteed level of financial support for anyone left behind.

If you're looking for a regular replacement income, after your own exit from the stage, there are *family income benefit* policies which, as the name suggests, are designed to provide a monthly payment to families. The policy is set for a specific number of years during which time your family will receive the benefit, either at a rate that doesn't change or else that increases to keep pace with inflation, depending on the details of your policy.

Endowments

The word has become tarnished by its associations with endowment mortgages, but life insurance is the natural habitat of endowments and the risks are different than if you're depending on their growth to pay off a mortgage.

Endowments work as a kind of mixture of straightforward insurance and investment, where you pay money in each month and receive a lump sum either at death or at some agreed date in the future. Unlike term insurance, you will get something back if you don't die.

The most common form of endowment is the with-profits variety, which means that money generated from the investment is ploughed back to make an even larger investment. The rate at which this grows will depend on the performance of the investments – and of course they can go down as well as up.

Endowments are often set across lengthy periods, maybe 15, 20 or 25 years, and the received wisdom is that in the long term stock market-based investments will outperform other savings, despite occasional setbacks, and will generate a decent return on your money. But these same wise owls also say that past performance is no guide to the future, so you pays your money and you takes your choice.

Payment protection

This type of insurance is usually attached to a credit agreement, whether it's a loan, a credit card or a credit deal on something you've bought. The idea is that if you can't keep up the repayments on this credit because you fall ill or lose your job then the insurance steps in and covers your monthly payment.

You can't really fault people for wanting to make sure that they're not over-exposed to their borrowings. But there are some sceptics who question the value-for-money of this type of insurance. Payment protection isn't cheap – and in some circumstances can amount to almost as much as you'll pay in interest. So there's no point bargain hunting for a loan if you then get stuffed by the add-on insurance.

There are also financial advisers who say that insuring one individual aspect of your credit commitments isn't really going to make much difference if you do unexpectedly find yourself without an income. If you're suddenly broke, out of work and facing a long list of creditors and still need to put food on the table, it's not going to be that much help to know that your payments on the dishwasher are covered. Instead your insurance needs should be looked at in a broader sense, protecting your whole income rather than one small aspect of your debts. You can buy *income protection* insurance which, as the name suggests, is designed to cover for your lost income.

Another aspect of payment protection that needs to be examined is whether you would be able to put it to use if you needed it. Policies usually require a number of weeks or months to pass before paying out and as soon as you do a day's work, they stop. So you have to ask yourself if you lost your job whether you would want to sit around waiting for the insurance to kick-in or would you rather go out and get another job.

Insurance wind-ups

- Small print: insurance is addicted to small print.
- Having to give so much personal information to get a quote.

- Insipid advertising. They don't want to scare us with risk, so instead we're swamped by soft focus schmaltz.
- Call centres: when you ring to get a quote and spend four days listening to irritating music.
- Online quotes: the computer always crashes after you've put in all your details.
- Insurers who take their existing customers for granted and don't pass on the rates used to lure new customers.

Ten things about insurance to dazzle your friends

- Theft is the largest single source of property insurance claims.

- 9 per cent of households buy private health insurance.

- 75 per cent of households have contents insurance.

- 10 per cent of motor and 15 per cent of household claims are estimated to be fraudulent.

- Two-thirds say they would cheat on their insurance if they could get away with it.

- 1 in 20 drivers is estimated not to have insurance.

- 20 per cent of mortgages are protected by payment insurance.

- 1.2 million homes are at risk of flooding.

- Insurers fear climate change could increase flooding.

- There is a moratorium until 2006 on insurers using genetic tests.

Modern money: 'It's like there's good insurance and junk insurance'

Karen, aged 41, works as a further education lecturer.

I'm sure that insurance has changed since when I was young. Or maybe it's how I feel about it has changed. There used to be insurance men, and they were always men, who came to the house and had all kinds of policies written out on elaborate pieces of paper, with all kinds of crests and clauses.

Now I've no idea of my insurers. I don't really have a mental picture of what they're like. I pick up a phone and ring round, or ring a broker, but they're all just phone numbers. It's never the same person who answers the phone – and I suppose really I don't even know if it's in the same building. And apart from price, I end up choosing insurance by my experience during those calls. There are companies which might have great insurance, but which I'll never use because of the stupid phone system. Dial one for this, dial two for that, dial three to listen to a load of irritating music.

I've never had any problems with claims, but it does sometimes seem very impersonal. And you could almost imagine ringing up and being told that they've never heard of you. Apart from the documents they send occasionally there is nothing to show that they are my insurers. If I wanted to see them in the flesh, I don't even know what city they are in.

When I say insurers, we have several, for the car, contents and life. And I've had travel insurance for trips abroad – and that has been particularly sketchy. It's always arranged in a rush on the phone and I'm never quite sure how much is covered. I'm thinking of getting an annual policy, and maybe look more closely at what it provides.

I'm not that bothered about all these types of insurance that people keep trying to force on you when you buy anything. It's partly because I'm never sure who all these insurance companies are and I'm not convinced that it's worth the extra money.

When you see how much it costs to take out insurance on paying back a loan, it just seems like another way of bumping up the direct debits. Even when you've almost paid off the loan, you're still shelling out all that insurance money. So in my own mind I make a distinction between 'proper' insurance, like car insurance, and the rest. It's like there's good insurance and junk insurance. The difficulty is telling which is which.

8

Debt problems – till debt us do part

Debt is a problem word, the label attached to borrowing when it goes wrong. Of course we're all debtors if we have mortgages or credit cards or loans, but we don't like to think of ourselves in the light of such a judgmental word. Lenders join in this conspiracy of optimism. While they like to send you letters about 'loan sales' they're not going to send you adverts for 'debt sales'. *Maybe we shouldn't talk about 'debtors', just very successful borrowers.*

> It's also part of our culture to borrow and to be in debt. We're laden down with a variety of loans – like waiters carrying too many plates, if we trip up, it's all going to come crashing down.

We are getting very good at borrowing. The speed of the increase in consumer debt is shown in figures produced by a government task force examining debt, which found that money owed through personal loans had increased between 1996 and 2000 from £24.5 billion to £40.4 billion. In the same period, credit card debts had risen from £11.9 billion to £20.62 billion.

This spiralling of borrowing has been matched by an increase in debt problems. The National Association of Citizens Advice Bureaux, which is on the front line of giving advice to people in money trouble, says that debt problems have risen by 39 per cent in four years. And it says that it is handling new cases each year involving £1.2 billion.

Such huge figures are difficult to imagine, but it's a total made up of hundreds of thousands of individual stories of ordinary people who find themselves trapped in what can seem like a nightmare of unpayable bills and the threat of losing everything into the black hole of debt.

Alongside the financial aspects of getting into serious debt, there are high emotional costs, with anxiety and depression associated with what can seem like losing control over your own life. Feeling that your home is at risk or that you're never going to be able to afford anything again strikes very deeply at our sense of security.

The scale of the problem shows that debt isn't just about a few extreme cases of money mismanagement. I've always been struck by how few steps away we all are from getting into financial difficulty. If you have a mortgage, imagine how quickly the debts would start to mount if you missed a few payments and how hard it is to catch up. And the whole world of money changes when you cross that invisible line and become a problem. I remember years ago, after I left university, I crossed this line with my own bank, and it seemed that overnight I had changed from being a valued customer with an overdraft into a debt recovery statistic. The tone of the letters changed, there were threats rather than requests, and there was the clear impression that I could either cooperate or else they were going to run the corporate steamroller over me.

There is plenty of advice available about sensible borrowing and the importance of not getting in too deep. But on the other side of the equation is the easy availability of credit and the expectation that we should buy first and pay later. It's part of our culture. And it's also part of our culture to borrow and to be in debt. We're laden down with a variety of loans – like waiters carrying too many plates, if we trip up, it's all going to come crashing down.

How do we get into debt?

There are plenty of moral connotations with debt, associations made with irresponsibility and stupid spending.

There is still a kind of Hogarthian caricature of debt as being a picture of booze, binge spending and a lack of self-discipline.

This would be a false image, according to the experts, who will say that the classic way that people get into debt is *a change in circumstances.* This can be a loss of job, divorce, the death of a wage-earning partner, illness or anything else that marks a sudden loss of income. It's a kind of financial whiplash. We're hurtling along the financial highway, earning money and borrowing money – and then there's a sudden stop to our income. But even though the earning stops, the spending commitments are still in motion.

Work out how much you have to pay in loan repayments each month – and then imagine that you had no income to cover these expenses. You might struggle through for a couple of months, but how long would your savings last? How long would it be before you couldn't manage the mortgage repayments? And once you start missing payments the interest is going to start running out of control and you're going to be spinning your wheels in mud. If you've got money outstanding on a credit card, personal loan, a credit deal for furniture and a mortgage – imagine if you didn't have money to pay any of them and they're all coming after you at once.

So to answer the question, how do we get into debt, the most typical answer is that people borrow like everyone else and suddenly life slams on the brakes. You could argue that people should have borrowed less, or that lenders should lend less, but that's too late for anyone who has got themselves into difficulties.

A psychological approach

While the most common type of debt will be the sudden loss of income, there are other more complex roots of debt. Money is about power and rewards – and there are people who use spending as an emotional pay-off, shopping therapy that makes people feel better about themselves. Although the immediate problem might appear to be someone spending a stack of money they don't have, it might really be about someone in an unhappy relationship seeking the kind of gratification they aren't receiving elsewhere.

Spending and borrowing can be *compulsive* – and debt advisers will have stories of people who have run up tens of thousands of pounds worth of debts, on credit cards, store cards and loans, with no means of paying any of it back. This money might have been spent on goods that were never even opened.

Like other forms of addictive behaviour, compulsive spending and borrowing can be accompanied by denials, self-deception and feelings of guilt. But money and credit cards are more likely to be a symptom rather than a cause of the problem.

I never said I was rational

Another way of looking at debt says that when it comes to managing money we're not rational creatures. Even though money management requires us to take sensible decisions in a sensible way, in practice we're often ruled by our emotions. Even though we have all the right advice, we might prefer to gamble than to play safe.

We often talk about money as if it were just a currency, but it's also a symbol in our lives, representing *power and independence,* or a lack of power and a desire for freedom. People can feel guilty about having money or ashamed of not having more – and all this emotional overhang plays a part in determining how we make decisions.

Jan Pahl, an academic at the University of Kent, produced research showing how people handle their money in a way that might seem eccentric – and that we're not guided by rational decision making. For example, she interviewed a headteacher who used cheques rather than debit cards because he could lie on the cheque stubs about how much he'd spent. You might wonder who he hoped to fool.

We've all played those kind of games at some time, trying to convince ourselves that an expensive holiday was in some way a bargain that could be afforded. Every month I get a credit card statement that makes me pledge to stop unnecessary spending and to begin a campaign to cut back on the outstanding balance. But somehow my resolve always weakens and I blur the amount I meant to pay back and all the good intentions get lost somewhere in the wine list. Of course I know what I'm doing, but on some level I choose not to know.

Take that a step further down the line and that kind of irrationality can get you into trouble. Jan Pahl's research also found a woman who spent up to the limit of her credit card and then when the limit was pushed up, spent up to that limit, as though they were giving her money rather than drawing her deeper into debt. This kamikaze approach to credit ended up with her having her home repossessed.

What can you do if you're in debt?

Every case of debt is going to be different and will benefit from individual personal advice. If someone is under financial siege it can be hard to be objective and think clearly, so it's important to talk to someone, such as the debt advisers at the Citizens Advice Bureau, who can offer practical support and set out a way of getting out of debt hell.

There is no single way of recovering from debt, but the type of strategy that advisers might suggest could include the following.

Working out the full extent of the problem and then contacting the creditors

This is the base camp of debt recovery, facing up to whatever is owed and perhaps for the first time admitting that there is a problem. Debt advisers say that they've seen husbands and wives who, in the course of counselling sessions, have for the first time confessed to their partners that they've been concealing debt problems for years.

Creditors will also prefer to be told the extent of problems and to be advised that a recovery plan is going to be put into action.

Prioritize debts

This is an important step towards deciding how to go about paying off debts, by distinguishing the most urgent debts – such as mortgage, rent, water, fuel and power – from those that can be put off a little longer. There's no point paying off your gym subscription if you're facing having your home repossessed.

One way of ranking debts is to think of *the worst possible consequences* of not paying. This is a kind of damage limitation process that puts into focus what's really at stake, whether it's getting the phone cut off, the furniture repossessed or getting a county court judgement against your name.

It also means deciding what's important for sustaining a financial recovery. If a car is needed to get to work, then having the car repossessed isn't an option. But you might be able to lose the dishwasher or the new DVD player.

Maximize income and minimize expenditure

Are there any sources of income that haven't been tapped, any benefits that are unclaimed or any ways of earning more at work?

Are there any savings to be made in outgoings, including ways of cutting the interest on outstanding debts? A debt adviser can be useful in taking an experienced look at budgeting and identifying ways of spending less and increasing disposable income. This will help to establish how much money is available for repayment and how much is needed for everyday living.

Draw up a repayment plan and negotiate with creditors

This can be worked out with an adviser, who can help in negotiations with lenders and creditors. This has to be a realistic and sustainable schedule for paying off debts, without recreating the difficulties that caused the problem in the first place.

This will mean finding a balance between showing a willingness to pay off creditors while protecting an adequate income for the debtor. Creditors will be happier with a reliable and consistent repayment schedule than an unrealistic attempt to pay back everything at once, which is likely to end up in arrears again.

Consolidating debts

Consolidating debts means combining all the outstanding loans in a single larger loan with a single monthly repayment. This sounds reassuring and is presented as being a way out of the debt trap. But think carefully before signing up.

What it really means is borrowing to pay off a debt, without tackling any of the underlying causes that led to the problem in the first place. Consolidated debts can sound cheaper because they have long repayment periods – but it's still money owed and will mean getting tied into loans that stretch out for years ahead.

If you are able to trade high rates of interest for low rates of interest, then that's an offer worth pursuing. But make sure that this is a step towards reducing your debts, rather than adding to your problems. Check to see if the loan is secured against a home, because the last thing that someone who already has debt problems wants is to put their home at risk.

There are credit companies that aggressively advertise these loans, presenting themselves as friends-in-need or even money advisers who are there to help consumers in financial difficulties. But cynics might see them as lending to desperate people who are already in trouble – and who need impartial advice rather than more debt.

When you're broke and casting around for a way out of what seems like a hopeless situation, taking out another loan can seem like a way of getting a reprieve. But it might be a better investment to tackle the existing debt and to take advice, rather than getting even deeper into debt and postponing the moment of meltdown.

Don't feed the sharks

There are plenty of people out there who see debts as a good business opportunity. You need money and you're in difficulty, and there are people, legal or otherwise, who will take advantage. This might be dodgy homeworking companies who promise good money, but pay a pittance. There are get-rich-quick schemes that are really get-ripped-off schemes.

It's worth being wary of the claims of 'credit repair' companies, which as the name suggests promise to repair your credit record, and so make it easier to borrow again. The organizations that hold credit references are strongly dismissive of the claims of these credit repair companies.

It's also a good idea to be cautious of bad advice. Just because someone says they are debt specialists, it doesn't mean that they won't try to sell you more loans or other products you don't need.

Of course the real sharks to avoid are the loan sharks, who still survive wherever people are short of money and without access to conventional forms of credit.

Debt warning signs

- You've begun to dread the post.
- You're overdrawn a few days after payday.
- It's getting worse every month.
- You can only afford minimum payments on credit cards.
- You have to put fuel bills and food shopping on to credit cards.
- You have to borrow to keep up with repayments.
- You're working overtime but it's all disappearing into debts.
- You're losing sleep and becoming worried.

Ten things about debt to dazzle your friends

- The average debt per household in the UK is £10,700.
- The average 'problem' debt has risen to over £20,000.
- Debt problems increased by 39 per cent in four years.
- Citizens Advice Bureaux received 1 million debt inquiries in a year.
- The level of secured debt has risen by 70 per cent in five years.
- Money owed on overdrafts is £5.7 billion.
- Money owed on personal loans is £41 billion.
- Money owed on credit cards is £21 billion.
- Debt is linked to depression and anxiety.
- Students graduate with average debts of £10,000.

Modern money: the debt adviser, Sue Edwards, Citizens Advice Bureaux

The National Association of Citizens Advice Bureaux sees a million people a year with problems with debt, of whom about 600,000 are in difficulties with consumer debt, including credit cards. These include a wide range of levels of debt, with some struggling with relatively small amounts, but with some people coming for advice after running up credit card debts of £30,000 to £50,000.

The most usual reason for getting into debt is not because of irresponsibility, but because of a change in circumstances that affects income. This might have been illness, redundancy, bereavement or divorce, any of which could leave someone with much less money than before.

If someone is committed to a number of regular repayments – mortgage, loans, car finance or whatever – suddenly having their income cut off is going to create a serious shortfall and it doesn't take long for the debts to mount.

There is much more credit available now than ever before and there is plenty of encouragement to borrow rather than save. There are adverts presenting borrowing as an attractive and easy way to increase spending power, with large sums of money available. Younger people are now growing up in a culture that accepts credit as a normal way of living and students have little option other than to borrow while at university.

Altogether the growth in credit has seen a corresponding growth in debt, and the Citizens Advice Bureaux are faced with an increasing number of clients who are trapped in the depression and stress of debt, feeling that they can't cope.

So what advice is given to people who get into trouble with credit cards or other types of consumer debt?

Each case is different, but in general debt advisers will seek to establish the extent of the problem and then to devise a practical way of beginning to pay off the debts. This will mean making a list of everything that is owed, all available income and spending commitments. Then advisers will help clients to think about prioritizing how they spend their money.

Debt advisers will also be able to negotiate with creditors about how much can be paid back, which might mean freezing interest or reducing monthly repayments. Even though they might have to wait longer for their money, Sue Edwards says that creditors are more amenable once they know that serious efforts to make repayments are being made.

9
Online banking – taking CTRL of your money

A couple of years ago you couldn't switch on the television or open a newspaper without hearing about how the whole world was going to be changed by the Internet. Online shopping, online share trading, online travel companies, online education, online newspapers – it was going to be online everything, where the old industries of bricks and mortar would be swept aside by the virtual economy.

> There are Internet bank current accounts that offer better rates of interest than many savings accounts.

We were heading for an online future, in which it seemed all the multi-millionaire entrepreneurs would be 18-year-olds who travelled to work by skateboard. These were the heady days of dot commery, when online companies that had barely launched were valued as being worth more than businesses with a shop on every high street.

Then dot com became dot gone and everything went into reverse, like film of an explosion played backwards. Companies that had acquired huge value on paper suddenly shrank and then disappeared. Self-important start-up bosses who had become online experts after attending a single conference suddenly stopped returning calls. Offices that had been recruiting hundreds of staff for a gold rush were suddenly reduced to a couple of part-timers and an answering machine. Companies that had been shovelling money into online experiments pulled the plug on Web sites, without ever having appeared to have known what they wanted from them.

Now that the Internet hype has receded, it's possible to see there have been changes that look like being here to stay. And one of these areas that has been changed forever – and for the better – is personal finance.

There are *Internet banks* which show no sign of disappearing. And there are millions of people who use traditional banks but who access their accounts on the Internet. These are developments that have become part of the everyday banking service.

Internet banks are much cheaper to run than banks with branches – and their expansion has been encouraged by the high rates of interest they can offer. There are Internet bank current accounts which offer better rates of interest than many savings accounts.

Accessing accounts online can also be very convenient for people who are always short of time. Once you get used to being able to check your account and pay bills online whenever you want, it's hard to remember waiting for a monthly statement and putting a cheque in the post.

Online share trading has also transformed how many people buy and sell shares. The bowler-hat factor, which put many people off crossing the threshold of stockbrokers, has been brushed aside by the Internet. And when online start-ups were in full flood, there were huge numbers of armchair traders who began to dabble in shares.

The uncertain fortunes of the stock market, and the plunging value in the dot com shares, have put off some of these newcomers. But the DIY share trading services set up by the high street banks and other specialists are still in place and it remains relatively simple for anyone to make investments. (And, as before, it remains relatively simple to lose money on investments.)

For almost any financial product the best advice is to shop around – and the Internet makes this much easier than before, with plenty of information available to help consumers make comparisons. The liquid pages of the Internet are the ideal medium for compiling and updating the kind of statistics useful for choosing between credit cards, personal loans or mortgages.

Choosing a credit card can be difficult when there are so many and when the advertising makes out that they're all the best deal in town. But if you go to a Web site such as moneyfacts.co.uk you can see the current top performers and make your own decision about what you want from a credit card, a loan, or whatever.

If you're looking for insurance, the Internet has increasingly become *the* shop window, letting you compare between instant quotes. AA Financial Services says that 45 per cent of quotes for car insurance are now provided online.

Financial services companies will now almost all have an Internet site, which you can use as a kind of electronic showroom to check out their products. But you can also use the Internet for more objective information. Watchdogs such as the Financial Services Authority have plenty of information for consumers available online. And there is also a move towards providing more specific data about products offered by banks and investment companies, such as comparisons of the charges attached to some types of ISAs.

But it's not all undiluted joy. You have to make sure that you know who or what is behind a Web site. It's not difficult to knock-up an impressive looking corporate Web site, even though the company behind it might be operating out of a back bedroom. Web sites that appear to be objective and offering advice to consumers can be plugging a particular product.

Credit card fraud is already widespread – and the Internet is another battleground between lenders and fraudsters. Although it's no more risky than giving out your details over the phone, people are wary of using credit cards online. Again it's important to know who you're trusting with your card, because you don't want to end up trying to recover money from a post box address in Nebraska.

Another downside to the world of desktop finance is that the Internet itself can be a pain in the backside. While people talk about surfing the net, it can often be more like hobbling slowly, as sites crawl into view or won't work without a load of extra software. I'm always aggrieved by how many sites seem to have been designed with no thought to how they will be used by the poor old punters. I'm sure they looked great in a demonstration at the PR agency, but if they take half an hour to download and then keep crashing, they're no use to anyone. In the long term, the basic speed and reliability of the Internet will have to be improved if this is going to become a truly mass market way of carrying out business.

Internet banks

You can usually tell whether a bank is an Internet bank by its name. If it's a short, quirky name, with no obvious association with a place or money, and it could equally be applied to a range of clothes or a type of after-shave, then it's probably an Internet bank. These include Cahoot, Smile, IF and Egg, all offsprings of other traditional financial institutions.

But the novelty factor is no longer a selling point, and Internet banks have to survive on their own merits. Their great strength is that they are very cheap to run and can tempt customers with *above average rates of interest*. Unlike traditional banks, with branches and the type of overheads that are acquired like barnacles over the decades, the new online banks have been able to run accounts for much less. They don't have a network of buildings across the country, they've started with a clean slate when choosing what services to offer and many of the day-to-day transactions are carried out by the customers themselves.

According to Cahoot, while it can cost a traditional bank up to £25 to process an application to open an account, an equivalent for an online bank is about 45p. These savings are part of the reason that Internet banks often feature prominently at the top of league tables of interest rates for current accounts. And their savings accounts can provide a decent rate of return for anyone wanting to avoid the risk of investing in the stockmarket.

The other reason that customers can still get a good deal from Internet banks is that *they want more customers*. Internet banks are still in their infancy, and they will have to offer rates attractive enough to win people over from the high street banks.

But Internet banks are not right for everyone. These are banks without branches, so if you like to call into your bank to chat about your finances, then these won't be for you. You'll also need to be fairly confident in using the Internet, because these kinds of account require a degree of self-sufficiency.

It's also worth remembering that in choosing an account, it isn't a question of only having one option. An increasing number of people have several bank accounts – and in particular Internet banks are used as second or third accounts. Even if people keep their existing accounts to pay the bills and for direct debits, they can open an account with an Internet bank as a way of accessing the higher interest rates available. It's simple to move money around between accounts, so setting up an Internet account is a way of getting the most from any spare cash, without the upheaval of closing the 'main' account.

Online accounts

Many traditional bricks and mortar banks allow customers to access their accounts through their home computers. And while many online services have stumbled, this type of home banking seems to have taken root and is steadily growing in popularity.

Barclays has over 2.5 million accounts that are accessed online, with the number rising each month. Increasingly these online customers are not the early Internet stereotypes of geeky young men, but are a far wider range of people, with a particular increase in the number of older people using the Internet to check their accounts.

So what kind of advantages are there to having your bank account on the Internet? And what kind of services can you expect?

The biggest advantage is probably *convenience,* in that you can sit down in your own home and check your accounts. Instead of depending on a monthly statement, you can have up-to-date information on your accounts as often as you like. It does really give a much clearer picture of the monthly patterns of income and spending.

When you don't know how much is in an account there is a great temptation to be optimistic and to trust to luck that there's enough. This is how I used to enter the overdraft zone, after trying to calculate a complicated set of factors concerning cheques being cleared and money being paid in. Internet access to your account stops that kind of guessing game, because it's very *easy to find out your balance.*

There is a psychological element to this, with many people feeling that Internet banking gives them a *greater sense of control.* There is something about banks that can make it feel as though you have to have their permission to move your own money. It is your cash, but it's locked up in their building. All the power seems to be stacked in favour of the bank. With an online account customers are on their own home turf, sitting at their own desk, on their computer, choosing when and where to examine an account. If you want to shuffle money around between accounts or to change standing orders, you can do it without asking anyone's permission.

The range of functions that can be carried out are relatively limited. You can *pay bills, transfer money, set up and alter payments.* But I suspect that the long-term impact of online banking will be changes to how we think about banks and bank accounts.

When all your banking information is laid bare on your home computer you tend to see more clearly what you're getting from your bank. And if you're getting a lousy rate of interest, it's staring back at you every time you turn on the computer. Considering that you can open an Internet bank account almost immediately, it's becoming very easy to set up an alternative to your own bank. Instead of a lifelong monogamous relationship with your bank, it suddenly becomes very easy to open another account. If this second

Online banking

account offers a much better rate of interest, then you can point your spare cash in that direction.

Instead of thinking of bank accounts as being carved in stone, the arrival of online banking has *made accounts seem much more flexible and in some senses more disposable.* When you look at your account details on your computer, the 'bank' becomes the branding at the top of the page and the level of service it provides you. If you don't like what you're offered, it's easier than ever before to open up another account.

Maybe bank accounts are going to go down the same route as credit cards, where people have found that the same service was being sold at very different prices – and consumers have chased the best deal accordingly. It might mean that people have several credit cards, but they're no longer passively going to stick with expensive cards. The interactivity of Internet banking is in itself a step away from the passivity which banks have always relied on from their customers.

Online share dealing

The emergence of online share dealing has helped to demystify the buying and selling of shares. In the process, one of the lessons that has been taught to new shareholders has been that investments can lose value – and that there is no certain path to making money.

What online share dealing has done is to make it easier for ordinary punters to carry out their own transactions, using the online service as an intermediary. You don't need to ring a stockbroker or even go out your own front door: it can all be carried out on your computer at home.

The most often repeated advice about anyone deciding to switch on their computer and start taking on Wall Street is that stock-market related investments are for the medium to long term and not the best way of using money you'll need next Friday to pay the gas bill. Not least because if your shares turn out to be duds, you might not have anything left on Friday.

It's also worth remembering that even if your shares are heading in the right direction it has to be enough to cover the cost of trading. You'll probably have minimum trading charges of £10 to £15 per transaction, so it's not worth buying and selling in 50 quids' worth here and 50 quids' worth there, because you'll be losing it all in charges. It's more likely that you'll need something approaching a thousand – and probably more – to develop a worthwhile share portfolio. But it does mean that if you want buy £500 worth of your favourite company, and maybe something more speculative, that you can carry out the whole transaction from your own computer or your desk at work. And with the information that comes with these services, you'll be able to track the progress of your shares over the months and years.

The process of buying shares on the Internet is itself straightforward. You'll have to open an account with a share dealing service, which you can do either through a specialist or a bank such as the Halifax, and then point your money in the direction of the shares you want to buy and press the button to go.

Online share dealing was also driven in the late 1990s by the apparently limitless rise in the value of Internet-related stocks. Everyone knew someone who'd bought shares in some Internet start-up that only cost 50p and were now worth £5. And it seemed as if this was an easy way of making money. Of course, with the benefit of hindsight, those shares are probably worth 25p now – and plenty of the first-time share pickers ended up losing rather than making money. If you want to trade in high-risk stocks with the hope of making more money more quickly, you have to be ready to accept the downside. And like any kind of gambling, *don't put on what you can't afford to lose.*

Without being too cynical, it's worth remembering the old saying that 'money goes to money'. While your £500 might generate some profit, the real action is about vast sums of money trundling through the money jungle, with each small movement generating a great deal of money for big investors and speculators. And for small-time punters, there's always a danger of being trampled by the big beasts.

Online window shopping

The Internet could have been made for financial window-shopping. All that number crunching and information gathering which you need when you're looking to borrow money or buy insurance is what the Internet does best. When people said that the Internet was a solution looking for a problem, then perhaps money was the missing link.

Mortgage hunting

If you're looking for a mortgage, the Internet can be useful in several stages of the hunt:

- showing what lenders are offering;
- showing what mortgage brokers are offering;
- calculating monthly repayments;
- comparing interest rates available;
- comparing discounts and special offers;
- comparing types of mortgage available;
- applying for a mortgage online.

You might still want to talk to a human being before agreeing to anything as substantial as a mortgage, but the Internet is a useful way of narrowing the field.

Many lenders also have mortgage calculators on their Web sites, which let you work out how much your repayments will be, depending on how much you borrow and the interest rate. And it can be easier to make these kinds of comparisons at home, rather than when you're with someone trying to sell you a mortgage.

It's also worth looking at the lenders' Web sites for advice. Of course, this is advice with a view to selling you something. But banks have got much better at providing objective information and explanations of what all the jargon means.

Personal loans

It wasn't that long ago that getting a personal loan from a bank meant dusting down the suit and paying an anxious visit to the bank manager. People didn't take out a loan, they *asked* for a loan, as though they were being granted a favour. And you couldn't just borrow money for any old reason, it had to be for a purpose as solid and respectable as the polished desk the manager sat behind.

In a few short years, the whole culture of lending has changed. With the arrival of the Internet and phone banking, you don't even need to go near a bank branch, and lenders are bending over backwards to make borrowing as straightforward as possible.

You can use the Internet to:

- compare interest rates;
- calculate monthly repayments;
- compare charges and conditions;
- compare payment protection insurance;
- apply online for a loan.

Insurance

Insurers have taken to the Internet much in the way that a decade earlier they moved onto direct selling on the phone. Unlike contacting the phone-line insurers, many people use the Internet as a way of researching quotes and cover rather than buying. After bargain hunters have done their homework, they might then ring round a final selection to get the best price.

Although some types of insurance lend themselves to direct comparisons on cost, such as the simplest forms of life assurance, insurance often isn't that easy to put onto an Internet league table. While credit cards can be ranked on interest rates or interest-free periods, it isn't so easy to make comparisons over car insurance or contents insurance. This is because there are so many variables and each quote is so specific to each applicant, depending on age, location, type of car, previous insurance history, value of goods and so on. In this sense there are still advantages to talking to someone when you're buying insurance, rather than clicking away online.

Money megastores

Whether you're looking for a mortgage, a loan, insurance, or you want to invest in an ISA, there are Web sites that provide for all these services and more. These are useful starting points for finding out about products and for getting an overview of what's available. These can either be pull-togethers that link to the providers listed, or else they can be showcases for the products of a pre-selected group of companies, brought together under a single banner.

The Bradford and Bingley's MarketPlace (www.marketplace.co.uk) lets you browse through the products of a pre-selected group of providers for mortgages, pensions, insurance and investments, in a kind of online shopping mall for personal finances.

A Web site like moneysupermarket.co.uk has updated details for products such as credit cards, loans, mortgages, ISAs and travel insurance. If you want to flick through the rates for over 300 credit cards, over 400 loans and 4,000 mortgages, this is the place. If nothing else, it can be a quick way of seeing how much difference there can be in the cost of similar products – and that someone somewhere is being badly ripped off.

For anyone wanting to look for a good deal, such Web sites are a great help. To gather the same volume of information any other way would take much too long, so be grateful that some other poor sucker is compiling all this data and that so far it doesn't cost anything to search.

Another blockbuster of a financial Web site, with an emphasis on investment, is from Interactive Investor International (www.iii.co.uk). It has a wide range of financial products that you can research or buy online. And www.moneyextra.co.uk is another Web site heaving with data and information about financial products.

In many ways these Web sites are addressing a long-standing challenge for financial services, which is, where do you go to buy them? You might go to a bank, but that's only going to be promoting its own products. You might go to a financial adviser, but even then you're not really getting the equivalent of browsing the shelves in the supermarket.

Internet sites are beginning to move into this gap, offering people a collection of products from a range of providers and showing them in a way that allows consumers to make a comparison.

Security

Any new technology worth its salt will provoke some kind of fear and suspicion. It happened to cinema, it happened to video and it will happen to whatever comes along next.

With banking or shopping on the Internet, the big fear is over security. The Internet is an anonymous kind of place, with no single authority in control, and people are afraid to send out their credit card and bank details in case they fall into the wrong hands. There are several sources of concern – that the details could be intercepted when they are being sent, and that whoever you entrust with your card and bank details could be hacked. And there is always a risk that you could be dealing with fraudsters who might take your money and give nothing in return.

The Office of Fair Trading gives some basic advice on how to limit risk when you're buying over the Internet; these tips include:

- Make sure you know who and where you're buying from, including a full postal address.
- Keep a copy of the Web page or advert.
- Make sure the Web site uses encryption to protect your credit card details (shown with a closed padlock symbol).
- Beware of scams – and 'if it seems too good to be true, it probably is'.
- Problems can be harder to rectify if you're buying from overseas.

Credit card companies are keen to encourage a sense that it is safe to trade online, not least because in the cashless world of the Internet, this is an area in which credit cards would hope to expand. There are initiatives by individual card companies that seek to upgrade security. These include American Express, which has devised a system in which you can buy online without sending your own card details across the Internet.

Spotting a scam

Of course, the scams that work are the ones that you can't spot. But the Office of Fair Trading also publishes a useful set of hints for some of the signs that should set off alarm bells if you're shopping online:

- companies which don't show an address;
- promises of 'instant wealth';
- hidden expenses and requests for fees;
- adverts that use TOO MANY CAPITAL LETTERS;
- adverts that say 'this is not a scam'.

There is a sense in which you can feel when something is dodgy. If you've never heard of a company and they've sent you an over-the-top offer or promise of bargains, then you have to ask yourself whether it seems plausible. If you send off money, consider how easy it would be to recover if you never hear anything back.

E-mail is a very quick way of reaching large numbers of people and when you receive your personalized promise of instant riches, you have to remember that it's probably in the in-boxes of thousands of other people. E-mail isn't bothered by national boundaries, and it's not unusual to end up on mailing lists from the USA or elsewhere. It could be a long walk to get your money refunded.

Here are 10 classic online scams:

- Pyramid selling.
- Chain letters.
- 'You've won a competition, congratulations'.
- 'Make a fortune working from home'.

- 'Free' holiday offers.
- Share tipping.
- Miracle cures.
- 'I need help taking money out of the country'.
- Buy a degree.
- 'Find out how to make a fortune by sending only…'.

Is it just the Bank of Bloke?

When online banking was first launched it was seen as being a very male preserve, appealing to the kind of men who hang around computer shops and who get excited about gadgets.

When Barclays introduced an online service four years ago, 90 per cent of accounts were held by men. The figure last year was 60 per cent, with the gap closing. Smile has tracked a similar shift away from an initially male usership. When the bank launched in October 1999, the ratio of male to female customers was 70:30 – the position after the first two years was 54:46 and heading towards parity.

Online banks are now attracting the so-called 'silver surfers': older people who are discovering e-mail and online shopping. At Barclays, one in ten of its Internet customers is over the age of 55, and Cahoot reports a considerable increase in the proportion of over-65-year-olds now signing up.

Psychologist Martin Corbett, senior lecturer at the Warwick Business School at the University of Warwick, says there is a well-established pattern for new technologies. The first adopters are usually younger males with a disposable income who buy into high-status gadgetry. After this first colonization of new technology has passed, it moves into the wider population. Mr Corbett points to the way that mobile phones have changed their gender image, from being seen as a distinctly male, high-value status symbol to becoming an object of mass ownership, grafted to the ear of every schoolgirl in the land.

Ten things about Internet banking to dazzle your friends

- 7.5 million people access their bank accounts online.
- Online transactions are much cheaper for banks.
- Sweden has the highest rate of Internet banking in Europe.
- The slowness of the Internet is a major frustration for customers.
- Internet banks are often used as second or third accounts.
- Egg was the target of the first Internet bank robbery attempt.
- One in ten customers checks their online account four times a day.
- Men are more likely to become 'bankaholics', repeatedly checking their account.
- Barclays claims to have the most online customers.
- Cahoot reported customers checking their account on Christmas Day.

Modern money: I can't remember what it was like before

Stuart, a 29-year-old catering manager, has been using online banking for 18 months.

> I don't think of myself as being any kind of anorak, but if I have the choice I'd rather be able to organize my own money, at home, on my computer, rather than have to ask the bank for permission to move my own cash. It's being able to carry out my own decisions that makes the difference.
>
> If I want to move money between accounts, I can get out of bed and do it straightaway, I don't need to write letters or make phone calls. And what's even more useful is always knowing where I stand with my accounts. It does make a difference. If I'm running low, I can stop spending. Or if there's a surplus building up in the current account I can move money into a savings account, where it can earn me a few more quid in interest. Although I suspect it's the control I enjoy as much as the extra money. It makes it feel like my money.
>
> When I first started working and using a bank account, I always resented the way that banks made my money feel like it was their money. If I wanted to get at my money I had to queue and ask permission. Now it's more hands-on. And the idea of paying a bill by writing a cheque and then putting it in an envelope and taking it to the post box now seems like another era.
>
> There are problems sometimes with Internet banking, but it's usually the fault of the Internet rather than the bank. If everything is taking too long or the line drops, it can be very frustrating. And somehow the slowness of the Internet has taken much longer to put right than people once seemed to be promising.
>
> I thought at one time that I might use online shopping quite often, but when I've tried I've had so many irritating problems with sites crashing and online shops that are all about flashy graphics and are hell for anyone to try to use. I'm always amazed that so much money can be spent on setting up an online store and then it doesn't even work when you try to use it.
>
> I don't know if I'll use more online shops in the future. But I think I'll always use the Internet for banking – and I

guess it'll improve and get more sophisticated in the next few years. Once you've got used to the independence, then it's hard to remember what it was like before. I used to go for ages without really knowing what my balance was – and then I'd find myself overdrawn. Now it feels like I'm much more aware of my finances.

In a way, being able to use my own computer for banking has made me more relaxed about my whole relationship with the bank. If I didn't like the service they were providing then it would be easy enough to open another account and try another bank. It's my money and it's my decision.

10

Excuse me, I'd like to ask you a question

1. Getting a grip

If you have a complaint about a bank or building society, the first port of call is your own branch. Whether in person or by letter, you should explain your complaint and supply any relevant information. Documents and evidence will be important in disputes, so make copies of anything you hand over in case anything is lost.

Banks and building societies should all have a formal complaints procedure, so if a dispute can't be resolved locally, you can then escalate the complaint to a higher level within the bank. And ultimately, if the bank can't resolve the complaint internally, it can be referred to an independent ombudsman.

The rule book for banks and building societies is the *Banking Code,* a voluntary agreement intended to make sure that customers are treated fairly.

British Bankers' Association
020 7216 8801
www.bba.org.uk

Building Societies Association
020 7437 0655
www.bsa.org.uk

Federation of Independent Advice Centres
020 7274 1839
www.fiac.org.uk

Financial Services Authority
020 7676 1000 (Inquiry line: 0845 606 1234)
www.fsa.gov.uk

Money Management Council
PO Box 77
Hertford
Herts SG14 2HW
www.moneymanagement.org.uk

Office of Fair Trading
08457 224 499
www.oft.gov.uk

2. Credit cards

If you want to check the current interest rates for credit cards and the deals available, the Web sites below have much useful and regularly updated information. They can really give you the bigger picture of the interest rates available. Every card claims to be a money saver, but here you can find out which are leading the field and which are wheezing along at the back.

If you want to know more about the credit card market, with background detail and statistics, the Credit Card Research Group is a useful starting point.

Credit Card Research Group
www.ccrg.org.uk

MoneyExtra
www.moneyextra.co.uk

Moneyfacts
www.moneyfacts.co.uk

Money Supermarket
www.moneysupermarket.co.uk

3. Mortgages

The rule book for mortgages is the *Mortgage Code,* which sets out how banks and building societies can sell mortgages. This has guidelines on how mortgages are marketed, the advice and information that are given to customers and what happens if these rules are breached. You can get a copy of the *Mortgage Code* from the Web site of the Council of Mortgage Lenders. If there is a further dispute, there is an arbitration scheme for the *Code.*

All the major lenders have Web sites that explain the types of mortgage on offer, current interest rates and terms and conditions. These are worth consulting for some virtual window-shopping. But if you want to see how lenders compare with each other, there are a number of useful Web sites that show the different rates on offer. These include Moneyfacts and MoneyExtra (see above).

Council of Mortgage Lenders
020 7440 2255
www.cml.org.uk

Mortgage Code Arbitration Scheme
020 7421 7444

4. Savings

If you have money to invest, you might want to take professional advice. This might mean talking directly to banks and finance companies, or consulting an independent financial adviser. These advisers can either charge fees or they can make their money from commission on products sold to clients. The IFA Promotion scheme can provide the names of independent financial advisers in your local area.

- If you think that you or a relative had a bank account and you've lost your documents and you're not sure where to look, you can trace these so-called 'dormant

accounts' through the British Bankers' Association or the Building Societies Association (phone numbers and Web sites above). This is a free service.
- *Ethical investment* has become a growing market in recent years, with customers opting to put their money into investment schemes that promise not to fund companies that damage the environment or operate in countries that abuse human rights. Information about ethical finance and specialist financial advisers can be found through the Ethical Investment Research Service.

Association of Unit Trusts and Investment Funds
020 8207 1361
www.investmentfunds.org.uk

Ethical Investment Research Service
020 7840 5700
www.eiris.org

IFA Promotion
0117 971 1177
www.ifap.org.uk

London Stock Exchange
020 7797 1372
www.londonstockexchange.co.uk

National Savings
0645 645000
www.nationalsavings.co.uk

ProShare
020 7394 5200
www.proshare.org.uk

5. Pensions

The Pensions Advisory Service (which is often known by its rather confusing acronym OPAS) is a useful starting point for anyone with a question about their pension – assuming that your pension company or employer hasn't been able to help.

OPAS has a free inquiries service that will try to explain your entitlement to benefits, obtain information from your pension scheme or help if you have not been able to obtain what you need, and try to make sure you receive the correct benefits. But it won't be able to advise on which pension you should choose. It's there for people who already have pensions and are having difficulties or, more often, having difficulty understanding how their pension works.

Annuity Bureau
020 7620 4090
www.annuity-bureau.co.uk

Occupational Pensions Regulatory Authority (OPRA)
01273 627600
www.opra.co.uk

Pensions Advisory Service (OPAS)
020 7233 8080
www.opas.org.uk

6. Borrowing

Whenever you apply for a credit card or for a loan, your past credit history will be checked, using the information held by credit reference agencies. The biggest in Britain are Equifax and Experian. You are entitled to see your own credit file, which they will post to you if you send them a request and a cheque for £2.

Equifax
Credit File Advice Centre
PO Box 3001
Glasgow G81 2DT

Experian
Consumer Help Service
PO Box 8000
Nottingham NG1 5GX
0115 976 8747

7. Insurance

There is now a watchdog for the insurance industry – the General Insurance Standards Council. This regulates how insurance companies operate in terms of sales, advice and service. There is a GISC code which members have to follow. If consumers think they have been mistreated, they can seek redress through a complaints scheme.

- If you think that you or a relative once had an insurance policy and you can't remember the details, there is a way of getting re-united with your money. The Unclaimed Assets Register holds details of unclaimed insurance, shares and savings schemes, worth a combined total of over £5 billion. There is a range of charges for searching the register, depending on the information you require.

Association of British Insurers
020 7600 3333
www.abi.org.uk

British Insurance Brokers' Association
020 7623 9043
www.biba.org.uk

General Insurance Standards Council
020 7648 7800
www.gisc.co.uk

Unclaimed Assets Register
0870 241 1713
www.uar.co.uk

8. Debt problems

The Citizens Advice Bureau service offers free, confidential and independent advice and is used by hundreds of thousands of people with debt problems. Advisers can help to find a way out of debt difficulties and can offer practical support such as filling in forms, writing letters and negotiating with creditors. For details of your local bureau, check in your phone book, or else the Web site has a directory of local offices.

There are other useful sources of advice, and it's worth checking any services available from your local authority. There are authorities that have debt advice information and support staff.

Consumer Credit Counselling Service
0800 138 1111

Money Advice Trust
www.moneyadvicetrust.org.uk

National Association of Citizens Advice Bureaux
Local bureau numbers in phone book, or through the Web site, http://www.nacab.org.uk/.

National Debtline
0808 808 4000

9. Money online

The Internet is a great research tool for anyone wanting to find out about personal finance. Almost all financial services companies will have their own Web sites and there are plenty of independent news services that provide analysis and commentaries on personal finance.

BBC News Online
www.bbc.co.uk/business

Financial Times
www.ftyourmoney.co.uk

Guardian Unlimited
www.moneyunlimited.co.uk

Money supermarkets

There are Web sites that pull together a large range of financial products from a variety of providers, covering areas such as mortgages, loans, insurance and investments. They are a useful starting point for seeing what is available and how much you might be expected to pay.

Find: financial services directory
www.find.co.uk

Interactive Investor International
www.iii.co.uk

Bradford and Bingley's Marketplace
www.marketplace.co.uk

Internet bank Web sites

www.cahoot.co.uk
www.egg.co.uk
www.if.com
www.smile.co.uk

Bank Web sites

www.abbeynational.co.uk
www.bankofscotland.co.uk
www.barclays.co.uk
www.halifax.co.uk
www.hsbc.co.uk
www.lloydstsb.co.uk
www.natwest.co.uk
www.rbos.co.uk

Conclusion

Who's afraid of the big bad bank?

So what have we learnt about money? Let's look on the positive side. It is possible to take charge of your cash and to overcome the sense of being powerless before the great turning wheels of the money machine.

Even though the banks and financial institutions have money and power, you have rights and you have choices, which you can exercise to your own advantage. The challenge is to get a grip on your own money and to make sure that it's working for you, whether that's in borrowing or saving.

It's all too easy to stand baffled before the jargon of money and let yourself be used as cash fodder for the big guns of the financial sector. If you want to pay over the odds on a mortgage, no one is going to stop you. If you want to be ripped off on a hire purchase deal, there will be lenders happy to take the money from you.

But if you decide to ask a few questions, carry out a little research and make a few calls, it is very possible to save money. If you look at your current credit cards, loans, insurance and mortgage, it's almost certain that you can find cheaper alternatives.

This is almost as close as life ever gets to easy money. There are often big gaps between the best and worst deals on the high street. And you might be surprised at the extent of savings you can make with very little effort, because lenders and mortgage companies will make it as easy as possible for you to switch to them. This will not actually add money to your income, but by reducing monthly payments, you will increase your spending money and give yourself extra financial breathing space.

If you repeat this shopping around process in another six months or so, you'll find that there are more savings to be made and that some of your former best buys have become not-quite-so-good buys. There's a cycle to this that usually applies: lenders want to find more customers and so offer a very good rate, and then once enough borrowers are on board the rate can drift upwards on the assumption that most people won't keep switching from lender to lender. And this is when you need to jump ship and look for another bargain.

If you want to keep ahead of the game, you don't need to be a total money anorak or even a statistics sleuth. Using the newspapers, the Internet or even just looking at the adverts will show you what's on offer – and then you can compare any new deals with what you have at present.

You can even try this out as an experiment: take charge of one single aspect of your finances – whether it's car insurance, credit card or a loan. Once you find the best deal for your needs, then you're setting a pattern you can repeat.

To continue with the sermon, we should also have learnt that there is nothing fixed about money and that you can move your mortgage, savings or bank account wherever or whenever you want if it's to your advantage. There are few rewards for loyalty in financial services – and if you leave your savings in a deposit account with almost no interest or you borrow using an over-priced store card, no one is ever going to thank you.

It's a strange truth that hundreds of thousands of people do choose to use store cards that have ridiculously high rates of interest when they could qualify for much cheaper credit cards. But just because some people are throwing their money away in unnecessary interest, it doesn't mean that everyone else has to follow.

On a less upbeat note, you should be honest about the scale of choice available – and recognize that the less money you have, the less choice you have. If you're on a very low income, then even getting a bank account or credit card can be difficult and you'll probably be offered the least attractive rates. The cheapest and most reward-laden cards are aimed firmly at the platinum end of the market, available only to those above a certain income.

Another depressing reality is that there are no magic wands available for hire – and as the Office of Fair Trading likes to say, if an offer seems too good to be true, it probably is. If you're in debt, it's going to take a long time to pay back what you owe and the amount you pay in interest will be sickening. If you're clearing a credit card, as we all know too well, it's a much longer and slower process than the quick-hit pleasures of spending. And even though you might be able to reduce how much you pay in interest, you still have to pay back what you've borrowed.

There are no instant-riches short cuts to saving. If you have a few hundred quid to invest, it's not going to turn into a fortune overnight. With interest rates relatively low in recent years, wherever you invest the money the earnings are going to be relatively modest. It's very unfair, but savings really work best for people with a stack of money because even in times of low interest rates, a great wedge of capital can still generate decent returns. As Winston Churchill supposedly said: 'Saving is a very fine thing. Especially when your parents have done it for you.'

This journey through personal finance should also have shown you that there are no definitively right or wrong decisions. There's no point putting money into the stock market if you can't stand any risk and can't afford to lose any of an investment. A low-cost loan might have great interest rates, but it's still a bad idea if the repayments are more than you earn each month.

It often comes down to a judgement, with the consumer left to weigh up the evidence. Should you get a fixed-rate mortgage? Unless you're a practising time-traveller, there is no one who can be certain. Interest rates have been low so far this decade, but such patterns can change quickly – and no one can really see around the corner.

However, an informed guess is better than an uninformed guess. You might not be right, but if you do some homework, your choice is less likely to be a disaster than if you just close your eyes and jump. Disaster isn't too strong a word when finances go horribly wrong. If your pension company collapses or your endowment mortgage leaves you with a large shortfall, then it can mean serious hardship and a great sense of injustice. And even though the financial companies spend millions on advertising, they have never really overcome the distrust that many people feel towards them.

There are contact details for regulators and watchdogs in Chapter 10 – and if you are worried or feel that you've been mistreated, then it's worth seeking advice. Banks, building societies and mortgage companies have regulatory codes to observe so you can check to see if they have fulfilled their obligations, and financial companies will have some kind of complaints procedures, which consumers can follow if they have a grievance.

It isn't easy to be assertive about money because many of us have grown up with an uncomfortable relationship with financial organizations. Even though we're customers of banks and insurers, we never really feel as though we're in control – and in fact there is often an underlying and unstated hostility between the customer and their bank. Even though it might be our bank, we don't necessarily trust it to act in our best interests.

This lack of openness and poor communication is often more of a problem for us, the customer, than anyone else, because it stops us asking questions and means we may buy financial products that are not to our own advantage.

All of which makes it even more important to arm ourselves with a little financial knowledge, even if it's just enough to stop ourselves being stampeded into unwise decisions. There are mortgage companies that pride themselves on being able to offer mortgages within half an hour of the customer's first call. That's all very convenient, but you have to think for more than 30 minutes about a decision that will be emptying your wallet every month for another 25 years.

So should you be afraid of the world of money? Not if you ask when you don't understand, refuse to accept

Conclusion

meaningless explanations and keep pressing for enough information to make a sensible decision. Then with enough information you can make plans that fit in with your own circumstances, whether it's saving for children, buying a house or whatever.

You should also not let your own opinions and experiences be overwhelmed by the voices of experts and analysts. You need financial services that are appropriate to your life, and even though advice is important, it's up to you to make the final decisions.

So be brave, don't sign anything until you're sure and if you find that magic wand, let me know.

Index

AA Financial Services   131
'affinity' cards   31–32
American Express   141
annual percentage rate (APR)   24, 25
annuities   75–76
Annuity Bureau   151
Association of British Insurers, contact details   152
Association for Payment Clearing Services   31
Association of Unit Trusts and Investment Funds   150
AVCs (additional voluntary contributions)   76

bank accounts   15
bank loans *see* personal loans
bank managers   8
Banking Code   147
banks   8–9
   bad experiences   8, 15–17
   case study   15–17
   complaints procedures   147
   Web sites   154

Barclays   133, 142
BBC News Online   153
borrowing   28–29, 83–99, 151–52
   car loans   94–96
   choosing loans   86–87
   credit cards   90–91
   credit unions   92–94
   mortgages   37–51, 92
   overdrafts   89–90
   types compared   87
Bradford and Bingley's Marketplace   139
   Web site   154
British Bankers' Association   147, 149
British Insurance Brokers Association, contact details   152
building societies, complaints procedures   147
Building Societies Association   147, 150
buildings insurance   107–08

Cahoot   132
   Web site   154
capped mortgages   43–44

161

Index

card fraud 30–31, 131
'cash advance' fee, credit cards 27
cash ISAs 61
cashback mortgages 45
cashpoint machines 15
   abroad 30
'Cat standard' 53
change in circumstances, and debt 121, 127–28
children's accounts 60
chrometophobia 15
Citizens Advice Bureaux 22, 47, 119, 123, 127–28
   contact details 153
codes of conduct 158
company pensions 71, 73–75
   final salary scheme 74
   money purchase scheme 74–75
complaints procedures 147
compulsive behaviour 122–23
consolidating debts 125–26
Consumer Credit Counselling Service 23
   contact details 153
contents insurance 15, 106–07
Council of Mortgage Lenders 49
   contact details 149
Credit Card Research Group 32
   Web site 148

credit cards 15, 19–36
   bad experience 35–36
   borrowing with 90–91
   case study 35–36
   'cash advance' fee 27
   charges 26–27
   choosing 131
   compared to other forms of borrowing 28–29
   debt 22–23, 33–34, 35–36
      psychology of 33–34
   fraud 30–31, 131
   interest rates 13, 24–26
   interest-free period 24, 26
   minimum repayments 27
   and online trading 140
   PIN numbers 31, 33
   reward schemes and incentives 27–28
   Web sites 148
credit checking 96–98
credit reference agencies 28, 97, 151
credit references 28, 96
credit repair companies 126
credit unions 92–94

debit cards 29–30, 32
debt 9–10, 65–67, 84–85
   and change in circumstances 121, 127–28
   consolidating 125–26
   credit card 22–23, 33–34

Index

debt advisers 124, 127–28
debt problems 119–28, 153
   causes 120–23
   contacting creditors 123–24
   local authority services 153
   prioritizing debt 124
   recovering from 123–25
debt warning signs 126
deposit accounts 58–59
   interest rates 13–14
discount mortgages 4–5
donation cards 31–32
'dormant accounts' 149

Egg, Web site 154
endowment insurance 113
endowment mortgages 37–38
Equifax 28, 97
   contact details 151
ethical finance 65
Ethical Investment Research Service 150
Experian 28, 97
   contact details 151

Federation of Independent Advice Centres 147
finance pages 13, 26
financial advisers 149
financial decisions 21
Financial Services Authority 63, 79, 131
   contact details 148
financial services companies, and the Internet 131

Financial Times, Web site 154
Find: financial services directory, Web site 154
fixed rate mortgages 45
flexible mortgages 45–46

General Insurance Standards Council 152
   contact details 152
gold and platinum cards 30
Guardian Unlimited, Web site 154

home banking 133
household debt 15
household income 15

IF, Web site 154
IFA Promotion scheme 149, 150
income protection insurance 114
Individual Savings Accounts *see* ISAs
instant access saver accounts 58
insurance 101–17, 152
   buildings 107–08
   case study 116–17
   contents 106–07
   endowments 113
   and the Internet 131, 138
   life 111–13

Index

    lost policies   152
    payment protection   114
    private health   109–11
    travel   108–09
insurance wind-ups   114–15
Interactive Investor
    International   139
  Web site   154
interest rates   47–48
    credit cards   13, 24–26
    deposit accounts   13–14
    Internet banks   132
    and loans   86
interest-free period, credit
    cards   24, 26
Internet   13, 26, 48–49, 106
    and financial services
        companies   131
    and insurance   131, 138
    money megastores
        139–40
    and mortgages   137
    online banking   129–45
    online trading   63–65
    and personal loans
        137–38
    scams   141–42
    security   140–41
Internet banks   56, 59, 130,
    132–33
    interest rates   132
    Web sites   154
Internet-related stocks   136
investment trusts   62–63
irrational behaviour
    122–23
ISAs (Individual Savings
    Accounts)   14, 60–61

    cash ISAs   61
    choosing   63
    maxi-ISAs   61
    mini-ISAs   61
    stocks and shares ISAs
        61–62

Land Registry   49
  Web site   47
life insurance   111–13
loan sharks   126
loans
    choosing   86–87
    and interest rates   86
    personal   88–89
London Stock Exchange   15
    contact details   150
'loser cards'   30
lottery   14

maxi-ISAs   61
mini-ISAs   61
money   5–7
    control of   8–9, 11
    living without   98–99
    and relationships   9–10
    saving   12–14, 155–56
Money Advice Trust, Web
    site   153
Money Management
    Council   148
money megastores, Internet
    139–40
Money Supermarket, Web
    site   139, 148
money supermarkets   154
MoneyExtra, Web site   148
moneyfacts.co.uk   131, 148

Index

mortgage calculators 48–49, 137
Mortgage Code 149
Mortgage Code Arbitration Scheme, contact details 149
mortgages 6, 13, 37–51, 149
 amount to borrow 46–47
 borrowing with 92
 capped 43–44
 case study 51
 cashback 45
 charges 39
 choosing 37
 considerations for borrowers 49
 default 47
 discount 4–5
 endowment 37–38
 fixed rate 45
 flexible 45–46
 interest 39, 40
 and the Internet 48–49, 137
 monthly repayments 41
 moving between 13
 repayment 42–43
motor insurance
 cutting costs 105–06
 no claims bonus 104
 specialist providers 104
 types of policy 105

National Association of Citizens Advice Bureaux 153

National Debtline 23
 contact details 153
National Savings 59
 contact details 150
no claims bonus 104
notice accounts 58–59

occupational pensions *see* company pensions
Occupational Pensions Regulatory Authority (OPRA) 151
Office of Fair Trading 141, 157
 contact details 148
online accounts 133–35
online banking 129–45, 153–54
 case study 144–45
 types of customer 142
online share dealing/trading 63–65, 130, 135–36
 and credit cards 140
 trading charges 136
OPAS *see* Pensions Advisory Service
Open-ended investment companies (OEICs) 62–63
overdrafts 16, 89–90
overseas transactions charge 27

Pahl, Jan 21, 22, 122, 123
payment protection insurance 114
pensions 6, 7, 11, 69–92, 150–51

165

Index

alternatives to 80
annuities 75–76
AVCs (additional voluntary contributions) 76
case study 82
company pensions 73–75
   final salary scheme 74
   money purchase scheme 74–75
group personal pensions 76–77
personal pensions 77–78
private pensions 70–71
stakeholder pensions 60, 70, 71, 78–80
work-based pensions 71
Pensions Advisory Service (OPAS) 150–51
   contact details 151
personal finance pages 13
personal loans 88–89
   and the Internet 137–38
personal pensions 77–78
PIN numbers, credit cards 31, 33
Plain English Campaign 7
Premium Bonds 59
private health insurance 109–11
private pensions 70–71
ProShare 150

rate tarts 25–26

relationships, and money 9–10
remortgaging and additional lending 46
repayment mortgages 42–43
reward schemes and incentives, credit cards 27–28
risk 102
Road Traffic Act 105

saving money 12–14, 155–6
savings 53–68, 149–50
   case study 67–68
   levels of risk 57–58
   types of 56–57
savings accounts 58–59
savings gap 15, 53
scams, Internet 141–42
security, Internet 140–41
sharks 126
'skimming' 30–31
Smile 142
   Web site 154
stakeholder pensions 60, 70, 71, 78–80
stocks and shares ISAs 61–62
store cards 29
supporter cards 31–32

term insurance 111–12
trading charges, online share dealing 136
travel insurance 108–09

Index

Unclaimed Assets Register, contact details 152
unit trusts 62
University of Kent 21, 22, 122, 123
utility and fuel bills 14

Warwick Business School 142
whole-life insurance 112–13
work-based pensions *see* company pensions